WITH WORDS

Young Writers' 16th Annual Poetry Competition

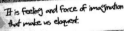
It is feeling and force of imagination that make us eloquent.

How can I not dream while writing? The blank page gives a right to dream.

YoungWriters

Staffordshire
Edited by Angela Fairbrace

 Young**Writers**

First published in Great Britain in 2007 by:
Young Writers
Remus House
Coltsfoot Drive
Peterborough
PE2 9JX
Telephone: 01733 890066
Website: www.youngwriters.co.uk

SB ISBN 978-1 84602 819 9

Foreword

This year, the Young Writers' *Away With Words* competition proudly presents a showcase of the best poetic talent selected from thousands of up-and-coming writers nationwide.

Young Writers was established in 1991 to promote the reading and writing of poetry within schools and to the young of today. Our books nurture and inspire confidence in the ability of young writers and provide a snapshot of poems written in schools and at home by budding poets of the future.

The thought, effort, imagination and hard work put into each poem impressed us all and the task of selecting poems was a difficult but nevertheless enjoyable experience.

We hope you are as pleased as we are with the final selection and that you and your family continue to be entertained with *Away With Words Staffordshire* for many years to come.

Contents

April Barton (12)   37
Lydia Swingwood (12)   38
Charlotte Burson (12)   39
Rebecca Webb (12)   40
Hattie Williams (12)   41
Adam Mankowski (12)   42
Natalie Moore (13)   43
Laura Whittington (12)   44
Natalie White (12)   45
Jade Hewitt (11)   46
Ashley Rogers (12)   47
Jack Quinn (11)   48
Laura Creaven (11)   49
Toby Mason (11)   50
Tilly Pugh (12)   51
Alyshia Haddon (11)   52
Ella Hodnett (12)   53
Isabel Wright (11)   54
Kate Mary Herrington (11)   55
Chris Stafford (11)   56
Laura Kelly (11)   57
Ian Robinson (11)   58
Stacey-Ann Smith (11)   59
Connor Bacon (11)   60
Faye Thomas (11)   61
Katie Banbury (11)   62
Laura Pugh (11)   63
Meghan Clarke (11)   64
Ellisha Perrins (11)   65
Sian Sweet (11)   66
Molly O'Connell (11)   67
Daniel Lowe (11)   68
Rachael Morgan (11)   69
Jessica Powell (11)   70
Tom Eaton (11)   71
Natasha Mandzuk (11)   72
Bethan Cooper (11)   73
Charlie Barton (12)   74
Jessica Rushton (11)   75
Sam New (12)   76
Lauren Quinn (11)   77
Hannah Barrow (12)   78

Scott Slater (11)	116
Carley Swift (11)	117
Caya McCarthy (11)	118
Ione Smallwood (11)	119
Zak Johnson (11)	120
Luke Mason (11)	121
Luka Reid (11)	122
Maisie Jane Baker (12)	123
Steve Whitehall (11)	124
William Mitchell (11)	125
Joe Baynes (11)	126

Sir Graham Balfour School

James McGraw (12)	127
Laura Isherwood (12)	128
Becky Haughton (12)	129
Jared Anderson (12)	130
Heather Benton (12)	131
Sophie Daltrey (13)	132
Alex Johnston (13)	133
Hannah Wallace (12)	134
Amy Casley (12)	135
Laura Rutherford (12)	136
Tom Bentley (12)	137
Emma Main (12)	138
Ryan Dodd (13)	139
Jade Streete (12)	140
Jessica Bowyer (12)	141
Dan Lakin (12)	142
Jemma Walsh (12)	143
Evan Saunders (12)	144
Holly Uttley (12)	145
Gemma Ingham (13)	146
Charlotte Rose Williams (13)	147
Josh Lewis (13)	148
Stephanie Willshaw (13)	149
Kelly Robinson (14)	150
Nick Miller (13)	151
Lucy Archer (13)	152
Callum Stevens (13)	153
Katy Austin (13)	154

The Poems

Starting High School

Starting high school, I felt like an ant at first,
One of the smallest
One of many.
A new exciting adventure,
New friends
New teachers
New people to meet.
Timetables, organisers, finding my rooms,
So many things, I'm a little confused.

Two weeks in and I feel much better
It seems like I've been here
Forever and ever.
Days go by quickly
With so much to learn.
Experiments in science,
Fractions in maths,
Learning to speak German
Is quite a task.

I'm not that ant anymore,
Because, as I learn, I grow
So on this adventure
I will continue to go!

Hannah Rowley (11)
Alsager School

My Sports Poem

I like to play football
Scoring goals is my aim
Put the ball into the net
To finish off the game.

I like to play cricket
Making runs is my aim
Catching balls and taking wickets
To try and win the game.

I like to go swimming
Doing lengths is my aim
Backstroke, breaststroke, front crawl too
Keeping fit is my game.

Ashley Edwards (11)
Alsager School

Magic, Magic

Magic, magic, it's all around,
Magic, magic, it's even on the ground!
Magic, magic, it's in the sky,
Magic, magic, it's how people die.

Magic, magic, it can't be found,
Magic, magic, it's why dogs bound!
Magic, magic, it's made up of electric,
Magic, magic, it can make you feel sick.

Magic, magic, it is really very old,
Magic, magic, it can't be sold,
Magic, magic, it's all over the place,
Magic, magic, just be careful, just in case!

James Hulson-Beech (11)
Alsager School

My Imaginary Friend!

His name is Almuh,
In his ways, he's very set,
He's sometimes grumpy,
But he's very much my little pet.

He has long pointy ears,
A small red nose,
He has great big feet,
But only three toes!

He's small and cheeky,
He is very, very funny,
He follows me all over
And has a big, fat tummy!

His mum is a fairy,
His dad is an elf,
Can you guess
What he is himself?

He's a pixie!

Jessica Gilmour (11)
Alsager School

The Wizard

Long pointy hat, a cloak as dull as a rainy day,
As he walks through the darkness of the night,
Move out of his way, or he might just cast a spell,
Not very nice, as that is how he will always be.
His house is an old rundown mansion filled with torturous stuff,
His driveway is as long as an airport runway,
His driveway is filled with gravel that looks like a snail's shell,
So if you walk down it, the stones crack,
Like a cockroach being crushed,
With trees that look rolled over, lined up by the side,
The sight is scary.
His servant, an ogre called Boris, is uglier than Shrek,
Doing anything the wizard says, it is a terrifying job,
He is green, slimy and is something you do not want to go near,
I hope you see this, as you throw up from the sight of it!

Harry Butcher (12)
Alsager School

Giraffes

G iraffes at Florida make me smile

I love it when their big blue tongues lick me

R ound outside they go and Busch Gardens they see

A pples they eat, licking their lips and all kinds of treats

F eeding the baby giraffes, children laugh and play

F riendly people watch and stroke, they wait until it's time to go

E xcellent rain washes them up for another day for luck

S ome calm down whilst others go to sleep for another day to play!

Chloe McAll (11)
Alsager School

In The Pool

I'm waiting
For the starting sound
And everyone is quiet
The water's rippling underneath
And the sound of beating hearts.

I'm swimming
Like a silver dolphin
Ploughing through the water
Freedom.

Splish, splosh
Loud splashing
People shouting
Silence
I'm underwater.

Sam Pickford (11)
Alsager School

My Friend's Dog

My friend's dog
Has a squid-wet nose,
Big brown eyes
And black and white spots
Right down to his toes.

He wags his tail
Like a windscreen wiper
Bouncing around,
Being hyper.

He is soft and cuddly
With a friendly bark,
We like to take him
To the park.

Jess Ayre (11)
Alsager School

Firework

F iring through the sky like a rocket
I ncredible noise
R oaring like a lion
E xploding into thousands of pieces
W ondrous colours fill the sky
O verhead the sparks
R ain down
K eeping the crowds of people entertained.

Peter Collins (11)
Alsager School

Black Magic

Dark magic is the evil that runs through people,
It is all the unfortunate events that happen day and night.
The ruler of chaos and destruction is black magic,
Dark magic is the unstoppable force that rules beneath us.
Dark magic is the cause for hurricanes and floods
And all chaos around us.

Josh O'Brien (12)
Alsager School

Hobbies

Sports are a popular source of amusement
Football, golf, swimming and hockey
Others hope to become a jockey.

Some participate, some just watch,
Others like following
What's top of the pops.

Cooking and baking I find fun
There's nothing like
A freshly baked bun.

Spotting trains
Is that entertaining?
I'd rather sit out whilst it's raining!

Some knit and others sew,
Others collect stamps
Why? I don't know!

Hobbies, pastimes, things that fascinate,
There are loads to choose from,
There's no need to wait.

Sarah Clarke (11)
Alsager School

The Sea

The shark-infested thriller,
The thing that makes you shiver,
Crashing waves,
Hidden caves.
The fishing shocker,
The sea gets hotter,
A sailor's dream,
The fish they've seen.
They are all so keen,
Different types of whales
And the wind that blows the sails.

Carl Dunning (11)
Alsager School

Witch

I'm going on a witch hunt,
What can I see?
I can see long green hair,
Red nails,
A long black cloak,
Jagged blue teeth.
She's wearing a pointed hat,
In her old, shriveled hand
She's holding a broomstick,
In the other,
She's holding a magic wand,
Oh no! what's she doing now?
I'm getting out of here
Before she cooks me in her cauldron!

Chloe Russell (11)
Alsager School

The Little Penguin

Little penguin gets up one day
And gets ready to go out and play
He plays in the park
Until it gets dark
Then he runs to the beach
And sits by the bay
To watch the shore
Wash away.

Megan Prendergast (11)
Alsager School

A Normal Day

The sun shines bright,
At the break of dawn,
I get out of bed,
With a long, loud yawn.

I eat my breakfast,
Go to school,
But today I've got swimming,
I love it in the pool.

Then I dry off,
Go to my next lesson,
But I still can't wait,
Until my next swimming session.

Rebecca Sheppard (11)
Alsager School

Magic!

M agic is glorious and empowering
A nd only witches and wizards can perform it
G lorious power rushing through your veins,
    can you imagine what it would be like
I t would be amazing, you would feel so powerful
C an you imagine being a witch or a wizard?
    I wouldn't like that!

Joanna Wootton (11)
Alsager School

Am I Old?

Am I old?
My hair has gone grey and curly
I look out of my window
But my eyesight is a bit blurry.
Am I old
Or is it changes?
Am I old?
I see yobs hanging around
And being cool
With a walking stick in my hand
They look at me like I'm a fool.
Am I old
Or just not cool?
Am I old?
When I walk past, no one says hello
I feel down and as if I'm on a go-slow.
Am I old
Or am I invisible?
Am I old?
I can't run anymore
My arms are weak
And my ankles are sore.
Am I old
Or am I old?
Am I old?
I can see wrinkles
Starting to appear
I feel cold and lonelier
By the year.
Am I old?
Really, am I?

Chloe Kershaw (12)
Brewood CE Middle School

Through The Eyes Of A Lego Man

Everything around me,
So colourful and bright,
But when I look at my surroundings,
No yellow men in sight.

I'm in my little red brick house,
Full of little chairs and beds,
But when I look next door,
No little yellow heads.

I'm now in the town,
Looking round all the corners and bends,
When a giant appears from above me,
With all my multicoloured friends.

James Rubery (13)
Brewood CE Middle School

So What?

I can't hang out,
I'm not like you,
People pity me,
For what I cannot do.
Just because I can't hear,
Going to school is what I fear,
I'm deaf, so what?

I only see things
In other people's eyes,
Why tell me,
Stop the lies.
I can't run
And cannot see
Why don't you leave me be?

In sports
I'm always picked last
My legs still work,
But not so fast,
I'm disabled, so what?

You do know I have a voice?
You can listen to me, you have a choice,
Don't laugh at me, or make me fear,
Now listen to me, come here,
I'm a child, like you . . . so what?

Jack Edwards (12)
Brewood CE Middle School

Where Do I Fit?

Where do I fit?
I just don't know,
When they reject me,
I'm at an all time low.

In the playground,
I walk alone,
Just because
Of my skin tone.

In PE I'm always picked last,
Just because I'm not very fast,
I get bullied and taunted everywhere I go,
I have no friends, only foe.

I'm not at all hip or cool,
When I act like it
I look a fool.

But there is always someone,
There to help amend
And I call that person,
'Friend'.

Robert Poole (13)
Brewood CE Middle School

I Can't, I Can't

I cannot see myself
I cannot see
So help and encouragement
Is what would suit me.

I can't remember anything
And I don't know why
No one will help me
And they are leaving me to die.

I can't have any fun
Because I am not like you
Playing games is just not me
Leaving me is all you ever do.

I can't do a lot
I can only stare at the moon
There is nothing better to do
So I hope I get well soon.

Elliot Beardsmore (12)
Brewood CE Middle School

We Are Still Young

We are not lazy, we are not dumb,
We are not slobs,
We are just normal people
Who aren't old enough to get proper jobs.

Leave us in peace while we hang around on the streets,
We are not here to annoy you,
We know the difference between good and bad,
So don't act like we're sad.

We are still young and free,
So we're not going to sit in the house and drink tea,
Not all of us drink, smoke or take drugs,
So leave us alone, we're not thugs!

Molly Andrews (12)
Brewood CE Middle School

My Deep, Dark Secret

I can't tell anyone,
Not my aunt, my dad or my mom,
I'll just pretend it's gone.

I can't take any more of this
Lying on the ground like the remains of a bomb
I can just see them laughing in the abyss.

I feel like a tennis ball
Swaying to and fro,
I feel sad and that is all.

I don't feel safe anymore,
I can't stand it at school,
I don't know why I'm not cool!

It seemed like things would never change
But they did,
They no longer say, 'Get lost, kid!'

It was strange when things were bad,
All these friends were not aware,
It seemed there was no one to care.

It wasn't easy to begin with,
But I made a friend
And gradually, my feelings began to mend.

It's much better now,
Today I joined all their games,
I now know everyone and all their names.

It's good I told someone,
So if this is your story, go on, tell,
Don't let your life be a living Hell!

Daniel Rimmer (12)
Brewood CE Middle School

What Do They See?

Most people see me, they just don't care,
I always feel left out, it's just not fair,
I see some old friends, they just giggle and laugh,
I'm not that different inside, I wish that time would turn back.

But everywhere I go, big sparkling pools stare,
I look away because in my heart I know they never care,
Being in a wheelchair for the rest of my life,
I'm not even a mother, girlfriend or wife.

There's no one here with me, I'm always alone,
I never check my email, I never check my phone,
I never wait for anyone, 'cause no one's coming home,
I wish it could be different, that time would still turn back.

The world through my eyes, is never the same,
It's not my fault and there's no one to blame,
If only I could see and my hearing wasn't so bad,
I'd be able to talk without being sad.

I am indeed blind and my hearing-aid is poor,
I wish I could see friends and family more,
I wish I could shop and see what I buy,
I wish I could hear the creatures in the sky.

Seeing the world through someone else's eyes,
Discovering their problems and how their time flies,
Helping and caring would help them a lot,
Then maybe their life would be much better off.

Emily Burns (12)
Brewood CE Middle School

Living Wonders . . .

Who brought us here? Why this planet?
Think of the meaning, why are we here?
We may as well live and just accept it,
So my questions, why aren't they clear?

The real question is, evolution or God?
Fate or science, you must choose,
Though these choices seem quite odd,
One you keep, the other you lose.

Sometimes we wonder what to believe,
Were we created from God's own hands?
We rarely respect what we receive,
Is fate destroyed by scientific plans?

The meaning of life is a powerful source,
Each of us has our future to live,
With a lack of fate we embrace our remorse,
To pass on that faith is all we can give.

The meaning of life is hard to tell,
Can we remember? Can we recall?
All we can do is to live our lives well,
Is there a meaning to life after all?

Sam Butler (12)
Brewood CE Middle School

Let's Go Back In Time!

Let's go back in time and change
Everything bad that we have done,
Let's go back in time and stop
Pollution, save the atmosphere,
We can save the world!

Let's go back in time
And take the opportunities that I haven't taken before
Let's go back in time and help save the people
Who are now dead
We can save the world!

Let's go back in time and help all those animals
Who are now extinct,
Let's go back in time and help the poor
Give them food, water and a place to live
We can save the world!

Amy Whatmore (11)
Brewood CE Middle School

Different

People look at me and stare,
They only see my wheelchair,
I can hear and I can see,
I'm always being treated differently.

People look at me and stare,
They don't see my lovely long hair,
I have feelings, I'm just me,
So please, don't treat me differently.

People look at me at stare,
They don't love and they don't care,
I'm disabled, I'm 33,
But why do you treat me differently?

Aimee Parker (11)
Brewood CE Middle School

What Is The Meaning Of Life?

What is the meaning of life?
Is it to find someone and get married?
Is it to have children
Or even to party all night long?
What is the meaning of life?

What is the meaning of life?
Is it to get a nice house?
Is it to buy a flashy car
Or even to become famous and get rich?
What is the meaning of life?

What is the meaning of life?
Is it to just be an average person?
Is it to get a good degree and get a super job
Or even to just be happy?
So, *live life to the full!*
Be happy!

Daniel Hampton (11)
Brewood CE Middle School

Why Am I Different?

Why was I born different?
Why am I not the same?
Why have I a disability?
Instead of Philip, that's my name!

I love all the people around me
I treat them all the same
I look to them for friendship
They look to me in pity and frown.

I am nineteen years of age now
And I understand your world
I can see your world through my eyes
I invite you to come and see mine.

I wish God would make me better
So that people would be my friend
I wish God would make me better
So that people would understand me.

Why won't you look past my disability?
Why can you not see Philip?
Don't you realise that we are the same inside?
When you laugh, I laugh, when you cry, I cry
And when you hurt, so do I.

Why was I born different?
Why can I not be the same?
Please look at me as Philip
Please try and learn my name!

Rebecca McLellan (11)
Brewood CE Middle School

The First Time!

The first time
I saw my kittens,
They were so fluffy
Just like a pair of mittens.
The first time
They saw me,
They sat on my lap purring
On the edge of my knee.
The first time
They went outside,
It was like an adventure for them
And they always went in a bush to hide.
The first time
They came in for a cuddle,
They were mucky and dirty
After they had been in a puddle.
The first time
They climbed a tree to the top,
They were crying and miaowing
Then they jumped down with a big *pop!*
And here and now
You can see,
All this time
They have had with me!

Georgia Haynes (11)
Brewood CE Middle School

Great Memories

I remember when I went to the water park,
Now I am just thinking of it in the dark.

There was water everywhere,
I was just wishing I was back there.

The slides were great, the waves were high,
I just wish we did not have to say goodbye.

Can't wait till we visit again,.
Till then, my memories will remain.

Grace Jones (11)
Brewood CE Middle School

Our World

Imagine the misery of people,
Who lose their children in war,
I want to stop this,
So there is no more.

Their mothers and fathers,
Cry all night,
Bang! Bang!
Now they live in fright.

A rumble in the distance,
There goes a bomb,
Oh no!
Everything is gone!

A wife's tears shed,
For her husband she weeps,
A child's fears,
Where will we sleep?

Look at us,
Me and you,
Who can stop this?
Tell me, who?

Ronnie Alipour (11)
Brewood CE Middle School

Look At Me

Look at me and what do you see?
A wheelchair and nothing else,
That's not all, I am like you,
I breathe the same air that you do too,
Please treat me as you would treat you.

Look at me and what do you see?
A blind man with his stick,
That's not all, I am like you,
I share feelings like you do too,
Please consider me like someone like you.

Look at me and what do you see?
Someone without a voice,
That's not all, I am like you,
I can play like you do too,
Please love that someone like you would love you.

Look at me and what do you see?
A default at the birth,
That's not all, I am like you,
I can give out kindness like you can too,
Please look at me how you would look at you.

Please look at me and see what you see,
A normal member of the human race,
No, that's not all, I'm not like you,
I treat other people as you should too,
Please treat them as you would treat you.

Georgina Hall (12)
Brewood CE Middle School

Why Are We Here?

The meaning of life - why are we here?
An endless row of questions.
From the start of life, to the end at death,
This question remains a mystery.
The universe
Always expanding, but into what?
Who made it and who will end it?
The Earth
What is its job? Why is it here?
How did it begin? How will it end?
Time
Always ticking away, but ticking until what?
What was there before time? What will be after?
Humanity
Why are we here? What is our job?
What is the point of life?
Nothingness
Is there time? Is there space? Is there life?
An empty void between life and death, who knows?
But here's a secret I'm about to tell
A key to the unknown
The truth is, no one has ever known and no one will ever find out.

Jordan Wynn (13)
Brewood CE Middle School

The Youth Of Today

The youth of today,
They sometimes say,
Are loud and rough,
In some strange way.

They mess around,
For all to see,
Destructive, bad mannered,
In front of me.

Hanging around,
Without a care,
Writing on walls,
That used to be bare.

The youth of today,
Have no respect,
I sit and think
And just reflect.

With nothing to do,
Trouble is made,
I don't really think,
This will ever fade.

The youth of today,
Are the next generation,
I say out loud,
With loads of frustration.

Tom Lloyd (12)
Brewood CE Middle School

Through The Eyes Of A Teddy Bear

You hold me when sad,
You talk to me when bad,
I wish I could live,
The life that you have.

I am furry and soft
And live in the loft,
My eyes glisten,
To hear you listen.

Eye to eye,
I see your face,
You raise my arm
And tie my lace.

You dress me up,
To look my best,
With a small bow tie
And a big fat vest.

My bedroom is big,
But not as big as yours,
It is like the world,
That opens new drawers.

Your TV is on
And you put me aside,
I become a loose figure
And don't feet alive.

I become dusty and damp
And feel all old,
I may as well be,
The same age as mould.

I am what I am
And that's just a teddy bear.

Lorenzo Troisi (12)
Brewood CE Middle School

When You Look At Me

When you look at me, tell me,
What you see,
An annoying teenager with a weird style,
Or a perfect person with a nail file?

When you look at me, tell me
What you see,
A teenager on a ramp
Or do you see me as a tramp?

When you look at me
What do you see?
A perfect little pearl
Or a little devil girl?

When you look at me, tell me,
What you see,
A posh person drinking tea,
Or do you see *me*?

I'm not invisible,
I'm a human too
And we don't say
Bad things about you.

You were teenagers once too,
So listen to us
And we'll listen to you!

April Barton (12)
Brewood CE Middle School

Who Shall I Tell?

My teacher, my mom,
Who shall I tell?
About the bully,
Who makes my life Hell.

Who can I tell?
What can I say?
About the bully,
Who hurts me each day.

I have a voice,
Which people can't hear,
Why aren't they listening?
I don't want to fear.

I'll pluck up the courage
And tell them today,
I can't handle this torment,
Day after day.

My teacher now knows,
What happened to me,
It's all going to stop,
ASAP.

They left me alone,
Today in gym class,
Nothing's now thrown at me,
No stones, no glass.

I've a spring in my step,
A smile on my face,
A warmth in my heart,
Now I forgive with good grace.

Lydia Swingwood (12)
Brewood CE Middle School

Away With Words

As I sit here in this dark, dusty room
I look out of the window at the bright full moon.
I wonder if I will be stuck here for the rest of my days,
Wishing my owner could change his ways.

The sun is up and it is morning at last,
I dream of my future and not of my past.
I dream of the day when it will all go away,
There is a knock on the door - is this the day?

I can hear them shouting and it's all about me,
They have had complaints and are here to see.
I race across the floor as they open the door,
They gasp as they see me, then there's no more.

They pick me up and make me all clean,
They find me a home, one that's not mean.
I love my walks where I can run free
And now I realise, they have saved me!

Charlotte Burson (12)
Brewood CE Middle School

Teen Beauty

When I was young I would sit there and stare,
At the beautiful models with their perfect blonde hair,
It's then I knew I wanted to be just like them
Exactly the same, with eyes like gems,
Long slender legs and perfect teeth,
Their standards of beauty were hard to meet,
But I knew one day when I grew to be a teen,
That would be me in that magazine,
I'd be worth a million or even more,
Me on the catwalks, my name they would call,
But as I grew older, I realised what real beauty is,
Not to be worth a million, but what lies within,
Beauty isn't everything and neither is fame,
So just be yourself, don't try to be the same.

Rebecca Webb (12)
Brewood CE Middle School

Bullying

I hate it when it happens,
I don't know what to say,
They hit me and they punch me,
Nearly every day.

I'm scared to go out to school,
I'm scared to go outside,
Just in case they come out,
Say 'you can't hide'.

How can I stop this?
Why do I have to run?
I just want to die
Can I find a gun?

What if I tell someone?
Will they tell me what to do?
Maybe I should stand up tall
And show them what I can do!

Hattie Williams (12)
Brewood CE Middle School

Through The Eyes Of A Bully

I am a bully
A bully of a school
I'm mean, tough and fierce
I use violence to solve everything

Everyone fears me
Even the teachers
I am always in trouble
And I *never* do my work

I am a bully
A bully of a school
I'm mean, tough and fierce
I use violence to solve everything

I'm a chav
Dress like one too
Waste my money on bling
And wear all new clothes

I am a bully
A bully of a school
I'm mean, tough and fierce
I use violence to solve everything

At home I'm abused
They hit me and kick me
And worst of all, they ignore me!
They are mean, horrible and tough
I *hate* it!

I am Spike
I need *help*
To stop my parents
Please help!

Adam Mankowski (12)
Brewood CE Middle School

Homeless

I walk alone,
Along the street,
All I have is my bag
And aching feet.

I've found a spot where I can sleep,
It's cold, but dry,
I try to be brave,
But I start to weep.

People stare as I lie on the floor,
They feel sorry for me,
As I am so poor.

When the winter comes,
I get so cold,
I hope I'm not here,
Till I am old.

Natalie Moore (13)
Brewood CE Middle School

Happy Memories

Ice cream
Wine gums
Frothing waves
Norah Jones

Seagulls
Kennack sands
Cornish camels
Cream teas

Wild wind
Gushing streams
Thick fog
Spider webs

Pink heather
Lizard Point
Chocolate milkshake
Skimming stones

Lifeboats
Candyfloss
Cold Coke
Swimming

Kynance Cove
Jellyfish
Big rocks
Salty hair

Cornwall.

Laura Whittington (12)
Brewood CE Middle School

Why Can't You Love Me?

I lie in my cot crying and hurt,
Wishing I had a voice,
Coming deep from my heart,
My mother, she hates me,
My father, he's gone,
Why does she harm me?
I'm not even one.
I don't understand what I've done wrong,
Can't you just love me,
Sing a bedtime song?
But no, you can't, you just hit me instead,
I hate my life, I might as well be dead!
So please will you stop
And show me some love
Because if you don't,
I'll be looking down from above!

Natalie White (12)
Brewood CE Middle School

What Is It Like To Be . . . ?

What is it like to be . . .
A football player
Speeding down the wing?
What is it like to be . . .
A football player?
Do you feel pleased
When you score goals?
What is it like to . . .
Play football?
It is great to play.

Jade Hewitt (11)
Brewood CE Middle School

I Remember

I remember driving my car
Going so fast, going so far
Racing round the track
Going so fast, going so far
Overtaking, holding back
Going so fast, going so far
Tyres burning, tyres smoking
Going so fast, going so far
The finishing line is in front - I've won
Gone so fast, gone so far!

Ashley Rogers (12)
Brewood CE Middle School

We Are Great

We are great at running, kicking, climbing and jumping
We are great at playing, working, clapping and climbing
We are great at talking, shouting, screaming and whispering
We are great at tennis, football, cricket and bowling
But the thing we are great at . . .
Is being ourselves!

Jack Quinn (11)
Brewood CE Middle School

The Feeling Of Loneliness

Have you ever felt alone?
The alone where you have no one,
Why do people leave me behind with no one
Not even someone I can call my 'owners'?
Owners, they don't care and love,
Or is it something that cannot change?
No love, no care from anyone!
Why is the feeling of loneliness
So cold and empty?
It's like being in the Antarctica
With no one to be seen
No food, no drink, nothing clean
It burns to think that no one likes you
It hurts to think no one cares
But at the end of the day
I might as well be dead!

Laura Creaven (11)
Brewood CE Middle School

Hurt And To Forgive And Forget

I looked at my parents,
They looked back at me,
I knew it wasn't to be.
They used to seem so happy,
But all they now do is argue,
Hurt each other even more.
My mum has just slammed the door,
My dad tries to stop her,
She has run away.
It was going to happen one day anyway,
I knew my mum would run away.
My heart is burning with upsetness,
My dad really doesn't care less.
I'm angry at my dad for letting this happen,
He's really upset me
And he knows it,
I'll just have to forgive and forget.

Toby Mason (11)
Brewood CE Middle School

An Untold Dream!

I woke up happy and delighted,
Looking around my room,
I walked over to my window,
The sky was a beautiful blue,
I saw trees so tall, birds so small,
Grass so green, flowers in bloom,
Sun so bright, clouds so white,
It truly was a wonderful sight!
I could hear my clock
Tick-tock, tick-tock,
Then *ring, ring, ring!*
I opened my eyes, looked all around,
I couldn't see a thing,
It was all a dream!

Tilly Pugh (12)
Brewood CE Middle School

My Life Being Bullied

I walked into school, so scared and afraid,
I wished this would never happen again,
I brought in the money they made me bring in,
I saw them turn round and give me a grin.

I shivered and shivered, terrified with fear,
Then they walked up to me and I thought, *oh dear!*
They got up to me and pushed me onto the floor,
I fell over and banged my head on the door.

It's home time now, time to pack away,
But I think those boys want me to stay,
So I run to the bus to wait in the queue
And the bullies run up to me and say,
'That's the end of you!'

Alyshia Haddon (11)
Brewood CE Middle School

Through The Eyes Of A Soldier

I wear a green suit and a tin hat
I sit waiting to hear a command
Then all I see is people looking at me
I feel ashamed, but they don't care
Because I am here to help my country

Every night I sit and cry
Thinking I could die
My hands are sore
I cannot eat

My sergeant stands and shouts at me
I block the sound out and ignore
He hits and shouts at me
He says I'm here to work and not to cry

I hear a bang
Now it's my duty
To defend my country.

Ella Hodnett (12)
Brewood CE Middle School

Keep Out! Private! For My Eyes Only!

B ullies, they spoil my day at school
U npopular, unhappy, they make me all of these
L ies, they tell a load of them. Laugh, it's all they ever do
L eisure, it's a hobby to them all
Y ikes! They're after me again. *Yell!* I try to save myself
I ce cream, they take my only one. Insults, words too rude to repeat
N asty, no need for explanation
G ive in, there's nothing left to say, it happens every day.

Isabel Wright (11)
Brewood CE Middle School

The Countdown

Five minutes to go,
Until the screams start
And the streets go silent
And Nagasaki falls lifeless amongst the mushroom of death,
When the houses and buildings collapse into rubble.

Four minutes to go,
I am looking around,
No one will know,
No one will see,
The small thing that will kill Nagasaki.

Three minutes to go,
Now it is too late,
It was always too late,
We will all die,
There is no question about it.

Two minutes to go,
No one will survive,
Everyone will die,
The earth will shake in anger,
When everyone and everything is wiped off the face of Nagasaki.

One minute to go,
Everything will go,
The startling light will rush over Nagasaki
And the mushroom will rise high,
Darkness will cover Nagasaki.

Zero minutes to go,
A loud bang shakes Nagasaki,
Mothers and children cry for mercy,
Nothing anymore is Nagasaki,
Everything is dead.

Kate Mary Herrington (11)
Brewood CE Middle School

A Dog's Eyes

Oh no, my owner's at the door
Look now, I'm shaking on the floor
He's just come through with his whip
He threatens to throw me in a skip
Now he's made my back sore.

He carries his weapons wherever he goes
Sometimes he hits me in-between my toes
He hits me 24/7
So I wonder what it feels like in Heaven
But after a bit, the pain goes.

I have more bruises than hairs on my head
Sometimes he throws me into my bed.

But all I can reply is: *woof!*

Chris Stafford (11)
Brewood CE Middle School

I Love You Both Still

You were both there,
When we needed your care.
We will all miss you,
But I never got to say,
'I love you.'

Nan, I'll say it now, but not again,
Though you don't mean it, I'm in pain.
Grandad, it wasn't long ago,
When I flooded out with tears,
Why did you go?

Grandad, I love you so,
Now that I know.
Nan, I love you so,
No more pain,
I love you both.

May the Lord Jesus be with you forever and always.

Laura Kelly (11)
Brewood CE Middle School

My Dog

My dog is a Jack Russell-cross
He has several lovely brown spots
He always tries to bite my dad
When his intentions go completely mad.

He always goes to my mum for dinner
When he feels he's getting thinner
He likes to give a little nip
Then we fitted him with a microchip.

When my dad takes him for a walk
On the lead he pulls, like a horse
He needs to go on a training course.

My dog runs away almost every day
Because he was a Sunnyside stray
Patch always has his mad half hour
Before he runs out of power.

When my dad throws his ball
He goes berserk around the hall
He is always meaner
When he attacks the vacuum cleaner.

Patch is like no other
So I love him like my brother.

Ian Robinson (11)
Brewood CE Middle School

Alone

I am Susie the sheep
Who just eats and sleeps
Standing in the field all alone
No one to talk to, no one to play
What more is there to say?

Now that I'm getting old
My little lambs have all been sold
I wonder what will be my end
No sheep here to be my friend.

I watch the birds flying away
Bleat, bleat, hello I want to say
I'm too old to be sold
That nasty farmer won't be told.

That is all I have to say
Of my life to the present day
My future is in the farmer's hands
So I won't make any plans.

Stacey-Ann Smith (11)
Brewood CE Middle School

The Teddy In The Corner

All I do is sit on this shelf,
I want to get down and walk by myself,
But with only one eye,
I sit here and sigh
And wonder why,
I'm destined to cry.

I've only got one ear,
So speak up my dear,
My lucky friend, Beth,
At least she's not so deaf,
Gets taken everywhere.

I like my owner,
Her name is Mona,
I like her friend
And the time we get to spend
Without my friend,
I've no time to spend,
Here I am going on the ride,
The ride down the back to hide.

Connor Bacon (11)
Brewood CE Middle School

Never Looking Back On Yesterday

As I walk out of my room,
I get this horrible feeling,
My heart starts beating,
I hear my name being screamed,
Why does it have to be me?

Scratches on my face,
Bruises on my waist,
What's going to happen now?
I walk down the stairs,
Wondering where Mom is,
Should I really be thinking this?
Does anyone even care?

As I walk into the kitchen,
Mom's there staring at me,
I walk over to her,
She pushes me back,
I fall to the floor . . .

Faye Thomas (11)
Brewood CE Middle School

Here, All Alone

I sit in the corner, hunched up, all alone,
Confused what to do, there's a ring on the phone,
I answer, I scream, I fall down on the floor,
Alive, but not well, someone opens the door.

Unable to see, unable to shout,
Up in my room, someone's wandering about,
I do not know who, I do not know why,
Unsure what to do, I sit and I cry.

Have they found out I'm here all alone?
Who is it? Who's there? They're still on the phone,
I leave it, keep quiet, see if they're still there,
I move and I sit by the corner of the stair.

Bang! and they've shot me, I'm there on the ground,
Never awake and never a sound,
Why and who was it? I will never know,
I should never have been left,
Here, all alone . . .

Katie Banbury (11)
Brewood CE Middle School

Survival

With my long brown ears
And my soft pink nose,
I hear the sounds of excitement
As I run from my foes.

Dogs snarl, men call,
Foxes stare as I almost fall.
Through the hedges and over the stream,
I pause to look back,
I've escaped and I beam.

To the valley of my home,
My family await,
I bring them food,
Before it's too late.

My burrow is safe, dark and deep,
My family secure and here we sleep,
This sunrise surprise, shock and fear,
What are the strange noises that we now can hear?

The huge metal jaws that tear at the earth,
The noise so terrifying, we huddle together,
Each bite destroys our homes we treasure,
Cruel, heartless men, too many to measure.

We run through the night, blind with panic,
Changing direction, we stumble, it's manic!
Out in the clearing, we realise our pain,
How can our lives ever be the same?

Moved on by Man, this life unfair
Yet still we survive, despite our despair,
A new home we make, but how long will it last?
Until Man comes again, and the dynamite blast!

Laura Pugh (11)
Brewood CE Middle School

Looking At The World Through Someone Else's Eyes

I look through her eyes,
She looks unhappy and sad,
She's scared and frightened
And people always say that she's mad.

When I look through her eyes,
I see her clenching her fists,
She looks like she's in pain
And she says she never exists.

When I look through her eyes,
I see tears of sadness
And then she's gone
Into even more madness.

When I look through her eyes,
I see the pain
And realise I must help,
So she never feels it again.

Meghan Clarke (11)
Brewood CE Middle School

Looking At The World Through Someone Else's Eyes

When I look through the little boy's eyes
I can't see anything, because he's blind.
All of his toys are hard to find,
Not being able to watch TV,
Only listening to the sound,
Walking along, not knowing what's on the ground,
That's what it's like to be blind.

When I look through the girl's eyes
I can see fine, but can't hear, because she is deaf,
She can't even hear her own breath,
She has to sign, instead of speak,
She wouldn't even hear the stairs creak,
When she tries to get to sleep,
That's what it would be like to be deaf.

When I look through the man's eyes
He is angry and upset, because someone has died
And can't get to sleep and is so very tired.
He goes to her grave to pay his respects,
He takes her some flowers that are called roses
With beautiful green leaves to cover all the weeds,
That is what it's like when someone sadly dies.

Ellisha Perrins (11)
Brewood CE Middle School

Bullied

I am being bullied
And I'm really getting worried,
I'm being punched and kicked
And beaten with large sticks
I am being bullied.

I am being bullied
And I don't know who to tell
All my friends have left me
It feels like I'm in Hell
I don't know whether to tell my dad
I am being bullied.

I've told my teacher
But that's made it worse
Because, today the bullies
Took off with my purse
I am getting bullied.

I overheard the bullies today
I ran away from school
I ran so far away
I wonder if I can make a friend
I can one day tell
I was bullied!

Sian Sweet (11)
Brewood CE Middle School

I Remember When

I remember when
I won my first trophy,
It was for a dancing competition,
Then I was best friends with Sophie.

I was proud of myself,
So was my dad,
I was proud of my dance partner,
We were both very glad.

I remember when,
I first started school,
I saw everybody with their friends,
I had none, I looked like a fool.

I was sad and lonely too,
But I am human, just like you,
So then I made a friend, two, three then four,
Now I'm not lonely anymore.

Molly O'Connell (11)
Brewood CE Middle School

If I Had A Time Machine

If I had a time machine,
I'd go back in time,
I'd undo the bad and make it good,
If I had the mind,
I might make one,
It would be fun,
I should do it now,
The first thing I'd do,
Is visit the part of the family I never knew,
I'd see what they're like,
I'd find out their names,
That's what I'd do with a time machine.

Daniel Lowe (11)
Brewood CE Middle School

A Blast From The Past

Why are we here?
I'll answer that question.

There was a very big blast,
Way back in the past.

It was made from a star,
About the size of a car.

From that day, some people say,
The blast happened in May,
Or even on Christmas Day.

Up on the grassland,
Even on the sand.

People on this day still ask the question,
Why are we here?

So I have answered your question,
So enjoy life to the full.

Go and have some fun,
In the golden sun.

Up on the green, green grassland
And on the light yellow sand.

Rachael Morgan (11)
Brewood CE Middle School

Going To The Past!

My brother running and screaming
What have I done?
My heart beating fast
He was calling me names.

I'd go back in time to change it all
I'd say, 'Sorry!'
I shouldn't have done it at all.

I'd put my arm around him,
We'd all make up and make things better,
That is why I'd go back to the past!

Jessica Powell (11)
Brewood CE Middle School

I Remember . . . The Bully

I remember when I was bullied
I remember when I didn't do anything
I remember when I came home from school
I remember when I refused to go to school
I remember when I told someone . . .

I told someone
I told my friends
I told my teacher.

It helped!

It worked
It's a memory now
And it won't happen again.

Tom Eaton (11)
Brewood CE Middle School

My First Day At Nursery

I remember when it was my first day at nursery,
I was very nervous, I felt like I was going to die,
I had a little sigh,
There was a good feeling in me though,
Our teacher was Mrs Potts,
She wore spotty socks,
I met lots of new friends,
The first time I saw them,
I knew they were going to be my best friends,
We learnt how to write our name,
Using a spelling game,
When we were on the playground,
We could run around,
It was the end of the afternoon,
Our teacher had had enough,
We picked up our bags and coats,
Then our moms picked us up.

Natasha Mandzuk (11)
Brewood CE Middle School

Alton Towers

A lton Towers is a great place to have fun
L aughing and giggling, but screaming
T orture I go through when I'm on the ride
O n the rides I'm shaking with fear
N ever stop screaming, I don't

T errible fear but I still want to go on again
O blivion, that's the worst, it just goes straight down
W henever I go on a ride it scares me to death
E very time I come off there's a thrill and disappointment
R ita-Queen of Speed, faster than any other ride
S o all the rides are scary but fun. Go there and have some fun.

Bethan Cooper (11)
Brewood CE Middle School

Global Warming

There was a planet
Called Earth,
Who's future
Created no mirth.

As the polar ice caps
Melt,
The devastation
Will soon be felt.

To save our beautiful
Planet,
Everything harmful,
We'll have to ban it.

Energy, we'll have
To save,
Or be overcome
By a great tidal wave.

The future is down
To us,
Do your bit,
Or don't make a fuss!

Charlie Barton (12)
Brewood CE Middle School

All On My Own

I sit in the corner, crying on my own,
I don't know what to do, I am alone,
Every time a teacher asks if I'm OK,
I suffer in silence and say, 'Yes, fine today,'
Every time the girls come up, I try to look away,
But there is no escaping, I get bullied every day,
There is no one there, but it's hard to walk away,
Hopefully, I can stand up
And be free one day!

Jessica Rushton (11)
Brewood CE Middle School

No Home, Alone

I'm homeless, my clothes are torn
I sell the Big Issue
People spit on me, thinking I'm an alien
I don't sell many magazines
My life's going nowhere
Can't get a job at the newsagents
I was brought up rough
I thought I was going to die
The other day I sold three magazines and bought a sandwich
Someone robbed the rest of the money
My dream is to get a job; can I fulfil it?

Sam New (12)
Brewood CE Middle School

My Name Is Tia . . .

My name is Tia, I am only three,
I have no toys and I cannot see,
I am waiting for Daddy to walk through the door,
I lie, so scared, on the floor,
Then I hear a car, Daddy storms in,
He hits my face, I cannot win,
Is it because I'm small? Maybe I'm just bad,
What else could make Daddy so mad?
He yells at me, comes close to my face,
He says it's my fault and that I'm a disgrace,
I say I'm sorry and I try to be nice,
I wonder how many whips I'll get tonight,
He grabs me by the neck, throws me down the stairs,
Somebody help me, this isn't fair!
I have too much hurt, too much pain,
I could run away, but he'd go insane,
I sit against the wall, bawling with shame,
My daddy's a monster, he needs to be tamed,
He kicks me and hits me, I'm lying still on the floor,
Crying and crying, him shouting more and more,
So I take my last breath . . .

Lauren Quinn (11)
Brewood CE Middle School

My Pony

Over the fields and far away,
My pony and I go out to play.
Didi's a bay, nearly seven,
When she jumps she reaches Heaven.
I love her and she loves me
And we live in harmony.
You are the best pony I've ever had,
Even though you're really mad.
Your tail is black, with a smooth kink,
Your long eyelashes never miss a blink.
Didi can jump very high,
Even though she's sharp and shy.
She's 14.0 hands and seven years old,
When she goes cross country, she's very bold.
I love you and you love me
And we will live in harmony.

Hannah Barrow (12)
Brewood CE Middle School

Orella

Orella is the best horse in the world,
Her mane is straight and is not curled.
She is 15.1 hands and nine years old
And her jump is very bold.
She loves her food
And enjoys being groomed,
She would do anything for you,
If you asked her to.
But hacking is her favourite of all,
She would take you for miles, with her head held tall.
She loves to gallop across open fields
And jumps the ditches with miles to spare.
Whenever I see a grey horse and rider riding in the sea
I imagine that is her with me.
Her gentle spirit, love and care,
Makes happiness bloom everywhere.
Throughout the time we have had her,
It doesn't seem as short,
Though I feel I have always known her in my heart
And we will never fall apart.

Lauren Cooper (12)
Brewood CE Middle School

Why Is It Me?

When I was 17, I was a ballet dancer,
But now my life is ruined by this cancer,
When I told my mom, she was really upset
And now it seems like something to regret.

My emotions and feelings are all mixed up in my head,
As I am awake here thinking on my bed,
Why is it me? Why isn't it a lie?
I can't believe it, I might even die.

It's getting to the point where I'm losing all my hair
And needing someone and some special care.

I am going outside into the street,
People are staring and looking from my head to my feet,
What are they staring at, whispering about me?
I feel that I want to hide away, behind a padlock and key.

I want to cry and let it all out,
I might as well, because there is no one about,
No, I'll keep it all in, I've got to keep strong,
Even thought I won't be able to for long.

I'm visiting the hospital at 4.30 today,
To see how I am doing and to talk to my nurse, Faye,
She said I'm doing great and to keep it up
And not to stress about the way that I look.

I'm getting better, but still quite ill,
But at least I know that the cancer isn't going to kill,
I am so pleased and really relieved,
That everyone has stuck by me and believed.

I'm raising some money for those who have cancer,
Because I am better and back being a dancer,
Cancer is traumatic and a horrid thing to have,
But I got over it and didn't go mad.

Zoë Thwaites (12)
Brewood CE Middle School

Me

I'm as naughty as a monkey
I'm as smelly as a pig
I'm as stupid as a goldfish
I'm as lonely as a spider
I'm as scary as a ghost
I'm as big as an elephant
I'm as flat as a pancake
I'm as slimy as a snail
I'm as hairy as a gorilla.

Toby Taylor (11)
Brewood CE Middle School

Wars

Wars, wars, why do we have wars?
People dying, crying,
Why do we have wars?
Wives depressed, moms are obsessed with them,
Dying to see their sons again.
But the children are crying
And their moms are lying
Because of them asking their moms
Where are their dads?
Because all that they can remember
Is him saying, 'If I am not back, be good for your Mom.'
But what about the bombs crashing down to the floor
Right in front of your doors
And people screaming and running out of sight?
You will be OK.

Adam Springthorpe (11)
Brewood CE Middle School

I Wish I Was Different

I wish I was different
I wish I could change
I wish I could be like you
Be just the same

I wish I could walk
I wish I could fly
I wish I could fly
Right up to the sky

I am a real person
Not just in a wheelchair
I would like you to see me
Not look away or stare

I am right here
Can't you see?
Don't talk to my owner
Please talk to me.

Kelly-Marie Roe (12)
Brewood CE Middle School

Invisible Identity

Remember the feelings, remember the days
The times you ignored me in those horrible ways
I'm not invisible, talk to me
Why can't anybody seem to see?

I'm just sitting here in my wheelchair
People stop, look and stare
They talk to my helper, not to me
I feel like I'm locked up with a padlock and key

I ask you God, hear my pleas,
I'm begging you down on my knees
Let me be free, pretty please,
Please just put me out of my misery
Or let me go, I'm having a horrible life
It's really slow
Let me go please, set me free
And let me be how I'm meant to be

I wish I could walk, run and fly
I wish I could go right up to the sky
Be my hero, be my healer
Get me out of this horrid four-wheeler
I'm not invisible, I'm right here
And I have been for longer than a year

Why can't anybody seem to see
The person in the wheelchair is defiantly me
Every night I sit there and cry
I feel like curling up to stay there and die

Remember the feelings, remember the days
The times you ignored me in those horrible ways
I'm not invisible, talk to me
Why can't anybody seem to see?

Charlie-Ann Edwards (12)
Brewood CE Middle School

We All Wish It Didn't Happen

(Written for all the people who lost their lives in the 9/11 attack)

It started as a normal day
I went to school and wanted to stay
When I returned, I was devastated to see
A bomb-load of destruction unfold in front of me
I sat on the sofa, stunned beyond my belief
Just three people had caused so much mischief
I paid my respects and I will do it again
But in a different way this time
With a piece of paper and a pen.

Daniel Guest (11)
Brewood CE Middle School

Civil War

Look at our young men dying
Look at our women crying
What has this world come to?
Blood spilling all over you!
Why, oh why, Lord?
Why have you given me this gift of using a sword?

Civil war, civil war
These guns are starting to be a bit of a bore
Whether you're black or white, rich or poor
Why should we bother with civil war?

Jonathan Sprague (11)
Brewood CE Middle School

The Eyes Of The Old

These amber eyes
Know all too well
But at the dawn
The cock will crow.

The hounds will rise
My stable mates stir
My stable groom awakes
I hear the door latch rattle
My stable companions greet their grooms.

The food buckets, that soothing sound
The smell of fresh hay slightly wafts around
I gradually eat, looking around
Suspiciously, I cannot hear a sound.

I look around, my groom's not there
Maybe he has gone, without a care
I want to go with them
Not left alone just because I'm *old!*

Alice Whittingham (12)
Brewood CE Middle School

The Devil Within

I cry at home in bed,
I cry in class at school,
She made me pay money,
I felt like such a fool.
It was Saturday afternoon,
I saw her in the street,
She looked me in the eye,
I could feel my heart beat.
She came closer and closer,
She pinned me to the ground,
I was so terrified,
Of that awful sound.
She threatened me with bruises,
She put me through the pain,
She kicked and punched me repeatedly
Again and again and again . . .
I felt so lonely, upset and beaten,
Why did it happen to me?
Am I really that unwanted?
They just can't let it be.

Georgina Bradshaw (11)
Brewood CE Middle School

The Day You Were Born

On the day you were born . . .
The rivers shone with a glisten that caught the eye
Of all passers-by
Machines moved silently just for this day
An old woman clambered out of her wheelchair
And walked freely through the streets on this day
Clocks stopped dead, just before midnight
To stay trapped in this magical day
An army ceased fire on their opponents
And shared friendship on this day
Planets stood still on their axis
So your arrival on this Earth could be recognized by all
You don't realise how much you have changed this world
On the day you were born, I thanked the Lord.

Nick Woods (16)
Clough Hall Technology School

Love Is . . .

Love is like a dream in which content lives everlastingly
Two mystical bodies come together as one existing sacredly
Flames of passion take control, under the spell of the unknown
Soul-searching relationships, successfully and beautifully grown
The recent meaningless life, which is now hoaxed
                         as I have found myself in the dark
You found me an angel from above, a bright star
                     which need not have a purpose to spark
Your beauty brought upon the plague of love, which is a black hole
                        in fantasy, for love is not a dream
It may cause a stir in the manner of mankind, as it contains
            many meanings in which some may not grasp, it may seem
The clocks tick in time with the heart of love and never stops
           in the mind and soul, although the madness can pursue
Love is unworthy to bind to happiness, as problems interfere,
            causing stress, strain and sadness and cannot be anew
Its mystique holds more than it wants and requires strength,
              honesty and responsibility with every aspect of itself
Love sparkles in some ways, others may not, it can alter
           the timeline of your future with its wondrous wealth
Shadow can easily pass through the deeper implication
             of it all, that of what it is, isn't, or could be
But an experience and life-filling enchantment, this is in the world
      of the universe surrounding us with the applications of it to take
               place, the heart sees what it wants to see
Does not ask questions about or if, it knows what it needs,
          what it wants and what it is and the pure good lies here,
               in which some it isn't found
With emotions so twistingly tangled the sensation to astound
       your happiness also belongs to me, as mine belongs to you
           and in our world will make a lovable reality of truth
              and commitments consisting in us two
Parting of the ways, but not from you, as I pledge myself
       by your special side, as even death could not dismantle
       this world we have chosen, as we would wait for each other
                in the light

Not to be disturbed by all the means, seeing our own reflections
in each other's eyes, hold the mind and soul of the reflection
to the eyes, bold and bright
Eternally combined to the person you want to be in the world
with for the rest of the existing time shared,
may love be forever flared.

Rhiannon Esmé Rhodes (16)
Clough Hall Technology School

Life As A Homeless Person

Life as a homeless person is different
Different than the average person's everyday life
For the majority of the time, it is hard
As hard as a diamond when trying to break it
Our lives are repetitive and constant
Which hurts when we are disrespected and insulted
We only want to live an ordinary, normal life
But as we sleep on hard floors at nightfall
And are forced to scrounge in cold streets in the day
We often wonder if our dreams will come true.

Ryan Thomas Smith (16)
Clough Hall Technology School

Leave Me Alone

I stand in a corner
Whilst they throw rocks
At me.
Well, at least it's better
Than being up a tree.
I imagine myself, exploding in
Fear and rage, even when
I grow another age.
Sometimes they chase me
Down the corridor.
With them beating me
More and more.
I considered
Committing suicide, when
My mum found me,
I lied.
I see them in my dreams,
'Leave me alone!' I
Would cry and scream.
'Leave me alone!' I
Would shout in rage.
'Leave me alone!' I
Would cry to this age.

Christopher Roberts (16)
Clough Hall Technology School

I Dream Time Is Frozen

I sit here silent on your mantelpiece, watching over the fire,
Working monotonously through time, feeling woeful and lonely,
The black brush numbers are running down my face: slowly,
With my feelings trapped inside my dead, wood oak
And my steel hands, all crooked and broke.

Tick-tock, I dream time is frozen,
Tick-tock, I dream time is frozen.

I wonder if you can hear my cries to the hour, every hour,
As my clockwork heart pounds one, two, three . . .
Like a drum, I'm desperate to break free,
Day and night and day, I'm not heard, as my silent roars
Are like a tame cat more and more . . .

Tick-tock, I dream time is frozen,
Tick-tock, I dream time is frozen.

You change my batteries; re-boost my low-life,
Polish my wrinkled, cracked face, why? I ask, do you keep me alive?
Is it because I'm your ticking slave?
I dream all day and I dream all night,
Knowing that I will lose this fight.

Tick-tock, I dream time is frozen,
Tick-tock, I dream time is frozen.

I sit here smugly on your mantelpiece, hovering above the fire,
For time has stopped, I'm feeling graceful and overcrowded,
The black brush numbers are dancing on my platform face
And my dead oak wood is alive again and again
And my hands of steel: spinning on their axis.

Tick-tock, I dreamt time was frozen,
Tick-tock, my dream is now over.

Jordan Forrester (16)
Clough Hall Technology School

Never Forgotten

Sometimes whilst it's late at night and everyone's asleep,
I sit and watch the stars twinkle by and I softly weep.
I remember all so clearly, as if it were yesterday,
When you would hold me safely and take all my fears away.

But time went by, I grew up fast,
I put all your memories in my past,
I became a stranger to you, I was such a fool,
I never thought for one second, that I could be so cruel.

It's too late now - I can't turn back the time,
But if you can forgive me, please give me a sign,
I didn't realise what I had, until you were gone,
Although I realise now, you made my life wholesome.

I need you to know, you're in every one of my thoughts
And without you here beside me, my life is distraught,
I need you, I miss you and I love you a lot,
I promise you sincerely; you'll never be forgot.

Katie Meredith (16)
Clough Hall Technology School

A Modeller's Knife

My trusty tool,
My greatest friend,
A sculptor's modelling hand,
A dangerous tool,
In the hands of a fool
That was my modelling knife.

I trusted it with my life,
How fickle a friend was that knife?
Cold and ferocious,
It turned on me; with no warning,
Its merciless blade slashed violently
And scratched my eyes, fatally.

Such a coward was that knife,
Hid in the dark,
Without any strife,
A hit and run, a masterful plan,
I couldn't get him,
But the damage was done.

Overwhelmed by fear and darkness,
Trying to familiarise myself to this new dimension,
My mind in a solemn state,
While my loving heart full of burning hate,
Weighed down with such a burden,
Like carrying the world upon one's shoulders,
Or being clung to by a billion black roses.

Stuart Hackney (16)
Clough Hall Technology School

On The Day You Were Born

On the day you were born
The rivers shone crystal clear
Machines moved in the lonely darkness of the midnight factories
An old woman rocked on her rusty chair, staring into the roaring fire
Clouds stopped dead
An army stood peacefully silent
Planets whispered
On the day you were born
So was I.

Andrew Quarmby (16)
Clough Hall Technology School

On The Day You Were Born . . .

On the day you were born
The rivers shone brighter than the stars
Machines moved gracefully the minute you entered this world
An old woman slipped peacefully from the Earth
To give her place in life to you
Clocks stopped to show your arrival
An army stood proud to salute you
Planets aligned because you're so special
All on the day you were born.

Kimberley Cope (16)
Clough Hall Technology School

Love Is . . .

Love is . . .
Everlasting, from the minute you wake up
To the hour the sun sets
When you cherish the time spent together
And enjoy the comfortable silences.

Love is . . .
A surprise, that jumps out on you when you least expect it
Feeling safe and protected wherever you go.

Love is . . .
The twinkle of an eye
The glimpse of a smile
The laughter and giggles
The moments you share.

Love is . . .
A feeling, a moment, a time, a place.

Love is . . .
The past, the present and the future.

Love is . . .
A mystery to everybody.

Kerry Smith (16)
Clough Hall Technology School

Love Is . . .

Love is . . .
A heart-filled feeling,
Trapped deep inside.

Love is . . .
A special connection,
Treasured and protected.

Love is . . .
A rose's beauty,
A snowfall's purity.

Love is . . .
Moonlight casting shadows . . .
On a stormy night.

Love is . . .
A blazing fire . . .
Strong and warm.

Love is . . .
A perfect smile . . .
A magical touch.

Love is . . .
Never being alone . . .
Never wishing for anything more.

Love is . . .
Us, together
Hopefully forever.

Emily Gilmore (16)
Clough Hall Technology School

If You Were

If you were the wind, I'd be the sail,
If you were the sun, I'd be a flower,
If you were a flame, I'd be the dark,
If you were a forest, I'd be the trees,
If you were an eagle, I'd be the sky,
If you were a jewel, I'd be the crown,
If you were a whisper, I'd be a secret.

Leanne Barber (16)
Clough Hall Technology School

Fame

To beat the rest
You have to be the best

To be queen of pop
You have to be on top

To be good with fashion
Choose your clothes with passion

Buy lots and lots of cool stuff
With blue ribbons and pink fluff

Try not to misbehave
Talk about the charity money you gave

Try to always look your best
No sweat pants or dirty vests

Stay slim, no junk food if you please
No one's going to like a celeb with a big bum and wobbly knees

Tabloids and paparazzi out for the scandal
Cellulite, affairs or socks with sandals

Stay strong no matter what they say
Or the press will have a field day

Whatever you do, give it an edge
Tell children to eat their fruit and veg

Choose an agent with lots of connections
With qualifications and high school elections

You need to be pretty
Smart, stylish and witty

Look good in every photo
And have a mobile, Samsung or Moto

Try to be sexy, but child-friendly too
Like Marilyn crossed with Winnie the Pooh

Try to get boyfriends every week or so
They often come and go

Get a small dog, kitten or bird
And call it Fluffy, Muffin or Truffles the Third

Have a nice car, house and garden
Never wear dungarees or Burberry/tartan

A message I leave you to think about:
There ain't nothing you can't be
You've got the whole world at your feet!

Imogen Dunmore (11)
Oldfields Hall Middle School

What I Would Do If I Was A Girl

Do my hair in groovy styles
Get to do my nails with files
I'd like to know how it feels
To walk around in high heels
My ears would be pierced twice
I'd cut my hair so I look nice
Buy clothes that are pink
Twirl my hair while I think
Put on lots of nice make-up
Get a golden retriever pup
My lips would be a ruby-red
I'd wear a nightie in my bed
Wear my slippers in the morning
Dress up nice when the day is dawning
And best of all, even better than a Snickers
Being able to wear, a big pair of frilly knickers!

Jacob Standen (11)
Ryecroft CE Middle School

The Things I'd Do If I Had The Money

Have a huge house with a big swimming pool,
Buy Microsoft, computers rule!

Make a new chocolate bar, 'Cream a la Crunch',
Buy all the poor a three course lunch.

Keep six tigers in a huge park,
Build a massive slide; you go down in the dark.

Buy Waterworld and make it better,
Bigger, faster and especially wetter!

Have a massive barbeque grill,
That's what I'd do if I had a bill(ion).

Kit Naylor (12)
Ryecroft CE Middle School

Wishes For The Disabled

If I had a wish
I would be able to fly
I'd fly so high and touch the sky

If I had a wish
I would be able to run
I'd run so fast, up to the sun

If I had a wish
I would be able to see
If I could see I would have seen that bee

If I had a wish
I would be able to hear
I'd hear all the things that I have always feared

If I had a wish
I would fly, hear, run and see
My life would be different, but I love being me!

Amy Land (11)
Ryecroft CE Middle School

Looking Through The Eyes Of A Footballer . . .

Oh no! I'm late, must get to training
We still have to go out, even when it is raining
Not looking forward to the match this week
The team we are against are a load of freaks
Big mistake, I'm on the back page
What can I expect - on this wage?
Free kicks, corners, they're my best
Sunday morning, need a rest
Like to play wide
Fans shouting and screaming outside
Went out with family for lunch
Paparazzi spying on us in a bunch
That's football for you!

Rosanna Dalton (11)
Ryecroft CE Middle School

What I Would Do If I Was God For A Day

Make money fall from the sky,
Give the hungry a slice of pie,
Rid the world of all bad,
Give all the orphans a dad,
Break up all the wars,
Make sure no one slept on the floor,
Freeze a lot of Arctic water into ice,
Brainwash all the terrorists so they're nice,
Take away all the bombs so the world's disarmed,
Stop little old ladies from being harmed
And at the end of the day I would play Xbox 360
(After smashing a PS3) all night,
Then I would rest, all right?

Calum Barnes (12)
Ryecroft CE Middle School

Things That Make Me Sad

Things that make me sad
And also drive me mad

Is when someone is kicked out at night
Or when someone loses their sight

Disabled people are also let down
Because they can't walk into town

The last thing that makes me sad
And also makes me mad

Is when people start to bully
And I don't find it funny

I think the world can be a horrible place
I would rather live in outer space.

Nathan Goodfellow (11)
Ryecroft CE Middle School

If I Lost My Mum

If I ever lost my mum
I would always pray up to the moon
And hope she would come back soon.

If I ever lost my mum
I would always speak her name
And never go insane.

If I ever lost my mum
I would speak to her every night
And never start a fight.

If I ever lost my mum
I would cry all day
And never go out to play.

But I haven't lost my mum
But will still think of her when I do
And hopefully, that will not be soon.

Erin Haig (11)
Ryecroft CE Middle School

The Bully

I could sense the fear all around,
The bully pushed a young boy to the ground,
Took his rucksack, took his lunch,
The bully used an almighty punch,
The bully ran at another kid
And at me, like he sometimes did,
I had to react very quick
And picked up the nearest stick,
The teacher called the bully's name,
The bully had subsided once again.

Jeremy Corbett-Marshall (11)
Ryecroft CE Middle School

What If Animals Had A Voice?

What if dogs really spoke their mind?
Would they say humans are always kind?
Would they still bark
Or chase their tail in the park?
Would they have posh names, like James or Mark?

What if cats were smart, not dumb?
Would they have four fingers and a thumb?
Would they eat out of a bowl?
Would they chase the garden mole?
Would they play football and score the winning goal?

So do you ever wonder, what if?
Imagine your pet just like this!

Rachel Allenden (11)
Ryecroft CE Middle School

Things I Would Do If It Wasn't For My Brother

Rest in peace every day,
Get bigger Christmas presents,
Always watch what I want on television,
Never get told off for what I didn't do,
Always choose what I want,
Never have to share expensive things
And best of all . . .
Always get the most expensive things!

Ben Harrison (11)
Ryecroft CE Middle School

A View From Far Away

Just look at those plush green forests
And the rolling and roaring oceans
All I have got is dust
Stop and admire the magnificent ice caps
Oh, how I wish I was there

Those things with two legs are so interesting
They have built so much and yet I have nothing
There are so many of the two-legged things
But only a few have come to me

I would have put up with the suffering
Just to get away from the loneliness here
If only for a while, I wish I was there
Oh, I wish, I wish I wasn't the moon.

Liam Turner (12)
Ryecroft CE Middle School

Mum

There are many mums,
But you are just the best,
You're kind and helpful
And you always clean my vests.

Yes, you are wonderful,
You really are the best,
Because you *never* really mind
When I make a mess!

Joe Mackey (11)
Ryecroft CE Middle School

Bullying

Sad, upset, pushed out, neglected
Go home crying to your mother

Down, gloomy, depressed, mad
Beat you up with their big brother

Angry, tearful, scared, left out
Take your lunch and dinner money

Lonely, joyless, cheerless, heartbroken
They point, they laugh, they find it funny!

Scott Slater (11)
Ryecroft CE Middle School

What Makes Me Angry?

Things that make me angry are what I see,
All the horrible crimes that all people fear.

I hate the killing of innocent people,
How can people be so feeble?

I hate the poaching of amazing creatures,
Then everything will go, all the wonderful features.

I hate the destroying of the masses of rainforest acres,
All those people don't give, they are just takers.

I hate the pollution humans make,
All that rubbish and grime that goes in the lake.

I hate the disgusting bullying that evolves,
Why can't it stop and just dissolve?

But life isn't always fair,
And that's the way it goes!

Carley Swift (11)
Ryecroft CE Middle School

Things That Make Me Laugh Are . . . ?

Things that make me laugh are
What I hear and what I see,
Things that make me laugh are
What somebody tells to me.

Things that make me laugh are
Comedians on the TV,
Things that make me laugh are
When I'm twirling around, free.

Things that make me laugh are
When somebody tickles my feet,
Things that make me laugh are
When someone falls off their seat.

Things that make me laugh are
When I see 'Big Brother's' Pete,
Things that make me laugh are
When I eat too much of a kind of sweet.

Caya McCarthy (11)
Ryecroft CE Middle School

I Am . . .

I am a big, round blob, floating around in space
I go around the sun in a slow and steady pace
Humans walk on my skin all day
Their feet pricking in me, they will pay!

My breath is polluted and full of bad gases
I am heavier than the moon and I weigh masses
Some of my warts burst and cause trouble
Some stand straight and don't even bubble!

Sometimes I will rumble and some cities will crumble
Sometimes I will blow so that people will stumble
Great rainforests and woods grow on me
And most of me is covered by sea!

Ione Smallwood (11)
Ryecroft CE Middle School

Ten Things Found In A Homeless Person's Backpack

A tattered picture of their family
A few items of filthy clothes with a few buttons missing
Sharp stones for defence
An empty packet of plasters
A piece of frayed string
An almost empty packet of dog food for their dog
A half-eaten, out of date packet of McVities biscuits
A leaking bottle of water
A battered piece of card with, *'please give money for the poor'*
Engraved on it
And 80p in two pence pieces.

Zak Johnson (11)
Ryecroft CE Middle School

Things I Would Do If It Wasn't For My Parents!

I would buy everything ever
I wouldn't be bossed around, not ever
I would play football all day
I wouldn't care what anyone would say

I would shout and scream
I would play for a rugby team
I would work and get a pay
I wouldn't care what anyone would say

I would sit and watch TV
I would run around and be free
I would do what I want all day
I wouldn't care what anyone would say!

Luke Mason (11)
Ryecroft CE Middle School

Why Do I Have To Be Bullied?

I got to school that morning
The same thing happened that happened every morning
I was held up against the wall
I had money taken because I'm not cool
Why do I have to be bullied?

In lessons every day
I have something thrown at me
A rubber, a pen and a pencil
Why do I have to be bullied?

At home today I sat in my room
And played on my PlayStation 2
I hardly ate any of my tea
Why do I have to be me?
Why do I have to be bullied?

Luka Reid (11)
Ryecroft CE Middle School

Kids Rules!

Chocolates and sweets,
Would be meals, not treats.

Funfairs and theme parks completely free
And kids respected, especially me!

School would be shorter, with no maths
And no homework with multiple tasks.

More pocket money to spend on stuff
And if the adults don't like it, then I say, 'Tough!'

There would always be a disco every night,
With lasers and strobes and really bright lights.

The rules may be silly and never come true,
But I really like them, what about you?

So there you go, rules written by a kid,
That's why they're crazy,
They were written by Maisie!

Maisie Jane Baker (12)
Ryecroft CE Middle School

Ten Things Found Under A Teenager's Bed

Under a teenager's bed you will find . . .

A half-empty bottle of Lucozade,
A chocolate cake I have made.

A flat football,
A picture of my dad, who is tall.

A big, blue box,
A season ticket with double locks.

A signed shirt from the Man U team,
A blue laser beam.

An autobiography of my nan
And a . . . *bogeyman!*

Steve Whitehall (11)
Ryecroft CE Middle School

Ten Things Found In A Poverty Home!

A dirty old blanket which they have to sleep in,
An old seat, all tattered and falling to pieces,
A broken net used to catch fish,
Smashed bottles all over the floor,
Just seven pence for all of them,
A pile of old magazines,
Bones on the floor from the fish,
Broken buckets to fetch the water,
A busted football which now they can use,
A broken cup, which they try to drink out of.

William Mitchell (11)
Ryecroft CE Middle School

In The Eyes Of A Bird

I fly on wings as wide as the sky
If people keep shooting me, I will die
I feed on pests, like rabbits and rats
So why do you keep killing me?

I fly on thermals in the sky
Without danger until you came along
With your guns and dogs
Why do you keep killing me?

With your bombs and tanks
You had war, caring only for yourselves
What brought this on us, may I ask?
Why do you keep killing me?

Well, it's time me and my friends fought back
The finches, the robins, the eagles and friends
Will soon rebel!

Joe Baynes (11)
Ryecroft CE Middle School

Colour Poem

The red flame of Satan,
The white light of God,
Each has a colour,
What does not?

One does not realise,
Just how precious colour is,
Without it, what would the world be?
Just dull, unappealing nothingness!

We live, we die,
We smile, we cry.
State of form or emotion,
Colours persist, throughout our lives!

Black is the lack of colour,
That's what many people believe.
I say different,
Colour is in anything you can see.

What many people may mean,
Is that grey is a dull colour, whilst red is fruitful,
But if you're unsure, if you have doubts . . .
Colour, is colour, is colour, is beautiful!

James McGraw (12)
Sir Graham Balfour School

A Day In The Life Of A Supermarket Trolley

Another day, another week, oh no . . .
The way the people push me round, oh no . . .
1000 grams thrown into my body,
Everybody thinks it's comedy!
Every day it gets worse and worse and worse,
Yesterday, there was a girl who left a curse.
She stubbed her big toe on the trolley,
She screamed out loud and then threw a wobbly.
Her mum was mad at her and embarrassed,
It got so bad, her mum became harassed.
Sometimes I do not get used, so I'm alone,
There's thousands of other trolleys, they moan.
I want something different and something new,
I can't believe it, there's more trolleys due!
I'm so fed up of the pouring rain,
But when they overload me, it's a pain.
It's so annoying when people bash me,
One day, this woman threw me into a tree!
Why do people not take care of us?
It's not like we can make a huge, big fuss.
Just dump us anywhere so we get hurt
And leave us all covered in litter and dirt.
Some people even take us far away,
It's really annoying, we don't know what to say.
There are some old ladies who treat us nice
And also in the night we have our friends, the mice.
We are very vicious and can be mean,
But once we get going, we are very keen.
Place us nicely in the trolley park or beware,
So come shopping if you dare!

Laura Isherwood (12)
Sir Graham Balfour School

A Doll In The Corner

I sit and watch
Lifeless all day
My eyes don't blink
My hair doesn't sway.

I cannot cry
No tears can fall
No emotion can be seen
In my glass eyeballs.

I sit and smile
I smile all day
I smile at people
And they smile my way.

I listen to everything
And hear most things
No sound escapes
Not even bees' wings!

When secrets are shared
And I am there
I hear them and keep them
And so does the teddy bear!

When the people are gone
And we are alone
Me and the teddy bear
Talk about our old homes.

So I sit in the corner
Every day by day
I watch people come
And go back their way.

Teddy may moan
But this is my
Home sweet home!

Becky Haughton (12)
Sir Graham Balfour School

Hallowe'en

Hallowe'en is the best time of the year,
Spooky ghosts, dark nights, all fill you with fear,
Scary pumpkin faces and bags of sweets,
Give it to them quick, or else it's trick or treat!

A test to see who has the best costume,
A skeleton's face or a witch's broom,
Laughing and giggling with your closest friends,
But you must do this before the night ends.

Go knocking on doors to annoy the old folk,
The reason Hallowe'en is such a joke!
Run away quickly, before they catch you,
Look out! Someone's around the corner, *boo!*

Your blood's racing and you're gasping for breath,
You feel like someone's half-scared you to death,
Feeling embarrassed, with rosy-red cheeks,
From being scared by a three-year-old freak!

You are so scared; you are ready to scream,
But that is just the fun of Hallowe'en!

Jared Anderson (12)
Sir Graham Balfour School

The Day I Turned Into A Boy!

Oh my life, what's going on?
Where has all of my hair gone?
I've searched the drawers, I've searched the bed,
But still no hair for my bare head!
Why do I suddenly dislike *pink?*
I just do not know what to think!
This is just completely weird,
Eewww look! I think I'm growing a beard!
I'll ask my dad if I can borrow his shaver,
But he might question my odd behaviour!
Oh no, I'm nearly late for school!
Mum is coming in, this isn't cool!
Oh no, what on earth will she say?
I mean, this doesn't happen every day.
She turns around and walks down the stairs,
But what shall I do about my *hair?*
My head has gone bonkers, I think I know why,
I . . . I think I'm a boy, but how? But why?
How on earth can this be?
What is going to happen to me?
I'm never, ever going to school!
I'll look like a complete *fool!*
Will I be a boy forever?
What if I'm never a girl again . . . ever?
I suppose it's not that hard, I guess . . .
I'll just have to try my very best.
Nobody will notice or know that it's me,
I'll just make sure Mum doesn't see me!
I open my wardrobe just to see . . .
A brand new skirt, just for me!

Heather Benton (12)
Sir Graham Balfour School

Birthday

Special day
Once every year,
Hip hip hooray!
It's time to try your first beer!

The chandelier is up
Now that you're 16 and nearly an adult,
Go on, have another cup,
No one's looking, it's not your fault.

The party has just started,
Now that you're in the room,
Let's crank up the tunes and get it really started,
The base goes *boom, boom, boom!*

Wow! It's time for the cake,
Turn the lights down so it's dark,
It looks like it took ages to bake,
I can hear a dog bark.

Sophie Daltrey (13)
Sir Graham Balfour School

Music

Music, one of the best things in the world,
A world without music, would be nothing,
So many types of music,
So many instruments.

A world without music, would be nothing,
Rock, rap, metal, classic,
So many instruments,
Guitar, piano, bass, drums.

Rock, rap, metal, classic,
Where did it begin?
Guitar, piano, bass, drums,
Legends are born.

Where did it begin?
We hear music every day,
Legends are born,
Millions of fans are screaming.

We hear music every day,
Whether it's music that makes your ears bleed,
Millions of fans are screaming,
The music settles the mood.

Whether it's music that makes your ears bleed,
So many types of music,
The music settles the mood,
Music, one of the best things in the world.

Alex Johnston (13)
Sir Graham Balfour School

Siblings

Siblings are annoying,
They come into your room,
They pester you and tell of you
And fill you up with gloom.

Siblings are annoying,
They look through all your stuff,
They hit you and kick you,
As if that isn't enough.

Siblings are annoying,
But in front of Mum and Dad,
They act like little angels,
When they're really, really bad.

Siblings are annoying,
They like to act tough,
But if you even think of telling,
They will start to get rough.

Siblings are annoying,
They moan and moan and moan,
Mum and Dad will tell us off,
Just because we groan.

Siblings are annoying,
You just want a way out,
It feels like they're blocking it,
Mum won't care, no doubt.

Siblings are annoying,
You have to scream and shout,
But then we might get grounded
And we won't be allowed out.

Siblings are annoying,
All the time, everywhere,
Then all of a sudden, they turn off the switch
And run free, without a care.

Hannah Wallace (12)
Sir Graham Balfour School

If I Ruled The World!

If I ruled the world, then it would change in many ways,
The world would be a brighter place.
New inventions, fat and thin!
No murder, or killings, or bad things.
Everyone would live in a mansion,
With glittering chandeliers inside!

If I ruled the world, there would be . . .
New animals for everyone,
A gigantic falcon that could take you wherever you wanted!
Everyone would get a million pounds every week,
For doing nothing . . .
Of course, I would get double!

If I ruled the world, me and my friends would get what we wanted,
Bad people would get punished,
Even if they didn't get caught.
Most things would be as bright as a button,
Colourful in many ways.

If I ruled the world,
Nobody could stop me . . .
From doing what I wanted to do,
You wouldn't have to go to school,
You'd be born with the education you need to get a good job.

If I ruled the world,
There'd be rabbits with trees on their heads.
Guinea pigs with worms for a nose,
All things wonderful!

But wait . . .
None of this will really happen,
I'm just plain and boring
And that's all I'll ever be.
No wishful thinking can change that fact.
I'll just sit here and be boring,
That's all I can do.
Plain and boring!

Amy Casley (12)
Sir Graham Balfour School

True Love

If you find your true love,
I'm sure you won't give them the shove.

If your love is pure,
You'll stick together, for sure.

Your love might be big or small,
Just give each other a call.

Your love will last forever,
As long as you're together.

If you're in love, you will fly
And feel like you could touch the sky.

You will always smile,
This will last for more than a while.

Everything will seem so bright,
Even in the darkest light.

Your heart will pound,
No other sound . . .

Your heart will be strong,
As if nothing could go wrong.

If your love is pure,
You'll stick together, for sure.

Laura Rutherford (12)
Sir Graham Balfour School

A Day In The Life Of A Shopping Trolley!

I start work at 7.00am,
Going along with my squeaky wheels,
A baby in my baby carrier,
Hitting my bar as she squeals.

They just chuck food in the back of me,
Without a single care,
Any old food for their Sunday dinner,
Turkey here, vegetables there.

When I finally get a break,
All that comes around,
More people walk in the shop,
Pushing me across the ground.

When my hard-working day,
Finally comes to an end,
I go outside to the freezing cold,
With my night, I have nobody to spend.

So all I can look forward to,
Is more work in the morning,
Or maybe something new!

Tom Bentley (12)
Sir Graham Balfour School

How Lucky You Are

When you are asleep in the morning sun,
Others are waking to a day of no fun
When you run around in the night or day
Others get a job with quite little pay.
When you eat three meals with all the mash
Others eat one meal with food from the trash.
When you take advantage of school and friends
Others work hard as a means to an end.
When you rip your clothes and tear them apart,
Others sell clothes from a scruffy old cart.
Just remember when you are all quite snug
Others are asleep, quite cold, with a bug.
There are people, far, somewhere else, sick, poor,
How lucky you are to have so much more.

Emma Main (12)
Sir Graham Balfour School

Champions League

The place to be is the Champions League,
The topmost position in world football,
Pace, skill, power, there's no place for fatigue,
To win this, you've got to give it your all,
Teams competing are in it to succeed,
Underdogs facing tough competition,
Trying their best to get into the lead,
For most, it is a difficult mission;
The people who are on top of their game;
Earn their rightful place in the last sixteen,
Searching for a place in the hall of fame,
For this, on a one goal lead, they can't lean,
Winning the League puts the world at your feet,
You can proudly say, 'We are the elite!'

Ryan Dodd (13)
Sir Graham Balfour School

A Day In The Life Of A TV Star

Today, on the set, it was really hard,
One scene that I was in, went very well,
My co-star was rubbish, but you can't tell,
One of my biggest fans sent me a card.

The big premiere is tonight, I can't wait,
I am not on time, oh, I will be late,
My dress is fabulous and my shoes too,
My necklace is diamond and very new.

The limo is not here yet, oh gosh no,
I hope all of the fans don't get too cold,
They will be of all ages, young and old,
I hope my lovely dress is not too low.

I'll be so nervous, I will not sit still,
My head will pound, I'll have to take a pill.

Jade Streete (12)
Sir Graham Balfour School

Guernsey Holiday

G reat experiences
U nbeatable beaches
E laborate gardens
R are, underground German hospital
N ice, irresistible food
S t Peter Ports is the capital
E legent, exciting island
Y es, we're going again

H erm is only a boat ride away
O ver-generous, platefuls at the hotel
L ots of fun to be had all over
I would spend every day in Guernsey
D elicate surroundings and ancient finds
A quarium by the sea
Y elling with tears on the way home.

Jessica Bowyer (12)
Sir Graham Balfour School

A Day In The Life Of A Frog

I wake up in the morning,
I'm as hungry as a horse,
My breakfast is a fly,
Yum, it's lovely, of course!

After my delicious breakfast,
I go on a little hop,
My mouth isn't quite clean,
Quick! Get a mop!

I find some long grass,
It's luscious, bright and green,
I see a lovely pond,
It's the best I've ever seen.

I see a lovely woman,
She's beautiful and pretty,
I already love her,
She's nice and gritty.

I love her
And she loves me,
We'll be together forever
And have some babies.

We've now got some sons,
They're really special,
They're now part of my life,
It will definitely be relished.

It's time to go and hide,
With James and the rest,
I love them all to bits,
They are all very much blessed.

We've now gone to bed,
Next year we'll relive it,
To all, goodnight,
Ribbit, ribbit!

Dan Lakin (12)
Sir Graham Balfour School

The Little Lost Child

I looked out through the windowpane,
To see a child crying
Out in the rain
Huffing and puffing, moaning and sighing
I stepped outside into the night
To find the child
Who looked a fright
But all she wanted was to stay in the wild
I crept up close till I was right behind
I told her not to worry
And told her not to mind
Took her home in a hurry
I tucked her up and told her to sleep
I sat down and sighed as I heard her weep.

Jemma Walsh (12)
Sir Graham Balfour School

The Voice Of A Slug

Hi, my name is Slugson Sluggy
I slime around looking muddy
I will slouch around and eat your plants
I look disgusting and smell like pants
Even when I sob and sulk
People squish me and sprinkle me with salt
My brains fly out with a splat
I make a cry, my bones go crack
My eyes go pop, my pupils flop
On the path, then people laugh
They point the finger and then stare
My guts just lay out standing there
My slimy skin is a popped balloon
By those bullies, stupid buffoons
I just hope it doesn't happen to humans
But unfortunately it does
But what can I do, I'm a slug!

Evan Saunders (12)
Sir Graham Balfour School

Why?

Sometimes I think . . .
Why is the sky blue?
Why don't we have three legs and why are we stuck with two?
Why do cats miaow and dogs bark?
Why do little children like the park?
Why is the grass green?
Why do we have a queen?
Why do we die?
Why do we smile and cry?
Why was television in black and white?
Why do we blow things up with dynamite?
Why do we have rainbows?
Why do we have ten fingers and toes?
The answer to all these questions is
No one knows!

Holly Uttley (12)
Sir Graham Balfour School

My Country, My Religion

I came here to get away
From a war never-ending.
With death so near,
My life descending.
Who are these people
And what are they saying?
In the back of my mind, I'm constantly praying,
My religion, my faith, is put to one side.
Every day is a battle, just to get by.
No one cares who I am, just of my race,
This country is confusing, with things you can't face.
I might not be like you and you not like me,
But we all have to share this country.

Gemma Ingham (13)
Sir Graham Balfour School

Today's Youth In The View Of An Elderly Woman

I think you'll find today's youth quite utterly amazing,
In a way that shows extreme misbehaving,
Maybe it's just me and my elderly age,
Although I do believe these yobs should be locked up in a cage,
The way they shout and couldn't care less,
Going around and leaving such a mess,
They drink and smoke
And annoy us old folk,
They graffiti and vandalise
And think they're wise,
When I was young I never behaved like such a brat
And I never did march around in a load of old tat,
It really is a disgrace,
That these youths constantly each have a grumpy face,
It honestly does make me feel quite upset,
That these youths are the noisiest youths I've ever met!

Charlotte Rose Williams (13)
Sir Graham Balfour School

If I Could Turn Back Time

If I could turn back hundreds of years
Or maybe one or two
This is what I would do my dears
This is what I would do.

I would stop all of the wars
I would stop the deaths
I might invent crazy new laws
Replace dinner ladies with chefs.

Forget boring old television
And old telescopes
I would make wacky smell-o-vision
And wacky smell-o-scopes.

I would meet kings and queens
And warn them of what's to come
Tell them of horrible scenes
So that they don't become dumb.

I would stop disease like bird flu
Anything's possible
So what would you do?
Make the world mad or keep it grey and dull?

Josh Lewis (13)
Sir Graham Balfour School

A Hooded Figure

A hooded figure
Coming towards me
I hear a small snigger
As deadly as a bee.

More are coming now
What is it they want?
Cats walk past, *miaow*
To them it is a taunt.

They are advancing
Advancing closer
Are they just bluffing?
Every one a sinner.

The gang is at me
What are they doing?
They're smiling smugly
Everything's blurring.

They are at my side
Walking past me quick
There's no need to hide
No need to panic.

Stephanie Willshaw (13)
Sir Graham Balfour School

Silent No More

I stand silent,
Wishing I could speak,
If I could, I would tell the world,
Exactly what I think.

On the outside I look so quiet,
I speak and nothing comes out,
But on the inside I could start a riot,
So would shout and shout!

If I could speak my mind
And also give my view,
I would search and find,
A way to be like you.

Sometimes I feel so alone,
When I am the only one who hears,
I don't like to moan,
But sometimes I shed a tear.

I hope and pray,
I could make a sound,
Some day,
So I could speak aloud.

I still have a task,
That hopefully one day,
They may ask,
If she could speak, what would she say?

Now all I can say,
Is I hope you appreciate,
That you can speak your mind
And may communicate.

Kelly Robinson (14)
Sir Graham Balfour School

Turn Back In Time To Adam And Eve

Let's give this machine a try
Hooray, it works
I am going, but why?

Adam and Eve, here we come
Soaring back in time
All we want is fun, fun, fun.

Adam and Eve are sent out of the garden
Because of the evil Devil
They may not end up in Heaven.

Now they are given a box to protect
They fight over who should do it
Then they elect without prospect.

She is so alone
Because Adam died
She wants to make a clone.

She needs to open the box
With lust and intent
She's thinking of being a sly fox.

God tells her no, no, no
She doesn't listen
I chuck the box in some goo and go.

Back to the future
No one is nasty anymore
Thank God I've save my own future.

Nick Miller (13)
Sir Graham Balfour School

Turn Back Time!

If you could turn back time,
What would you change?
The result of your last football match
Or when your parents chose your name.

When you dropped out of drama club,
When you ruined your best ever shoes;
The ball that smashed next door's window,
Or those dodgy friends that you wish you never knew.

When you didn't revise for your end of year test,
Or the clothes you wore on your first date;
When you were younger, that horrible haircut,
When at your best friend's party, you arrived twenty minutes late.

How you always forgot your boyfriend's birthday,
The time you were away for the first day of school;
How you sucked your thumb until the age of nine,
When you were caught drowning your brother
In the local swimming pool.

When you quit playing the violin,
How you stayed off school when you weren't actually sick;
The way you always left your homework to the last minute,
Those annoying chavs, who always took the mick.

But as well as those bad times,
All those times that made you want to sing;
If I could turn back time,
I wouldn't change a thing!

Lucy Archer (13)
Sir Graham Balfour School

Time Lord

If I could turn back the hands of time
I'll tell you about it in this little rhyme.
I would not do what I was told to
I would put stink bombs in my dad's shoe.
I would eat all the cake in the house
I would play tennis with my sister's mouse.
When my mum said get to your room
I'd fly through my window on a magic broom.
If I could turn back the hands of time
I'd eradicate all sorts of crime.
My great, great grandad from World War I
Wouldn't have died at twenty-one.
All of these things I could do
If only I was Doctor Who!

Callum Stevens (13)
Sir Graham Balfour School

If I Could Turn Back Time

If I could turn back time,
I wouldn't have been nasty;
I wouldn't have hurt my brother.

If I could turn back time,
I wouldn't have been cheeky;
I wouldn't have shouted at my mother.

If I could turn back time,
I wouldn't have been naughty;
I wouldn't have ignored my teacher.

So if I could turn back time
I would have been born an angel!

Katy Austin (13)
Sir Graham Balfour School

Back In Time

If I could go back in time,
Here's what I'd do.
Well, I'd go back,
To nineteen ninety-two!

This was the year I was born
What fun it would be
To see what was going on,
In British history.

'Annus horribilis' said the Queen,
Princess Anne divorced,
Another marriage fell apart,
Duke and Duchess of York.

Olympic Games in Barcelona,
But England never won,
We got some medals
And a prize of the red-hot sun.

The longest Channel Tunnel,
From England to France,
Under the sea is planned,
Travel through in a trance.

I'm glad I was a baby,
It doesn't sound that nice.
I'd rather be here now,
Where I can get advice.

Lucy Swaries (14)
Sir Graham Balfour School

If I Could Turn Back Time

If I could turn back time
I would go to a secluded space
Further than the birth of the Earth
And right off the face
Of this crime we call turf.

Nowhere near popular culture
Or the vulture
Of advertisement
Back further than the word freedom
All the way back to Eden
With simple alignments.

When pain was but a nightmare
And trees and pains grew without a care
When animals lived in harmony with you and me
And we should share
All that was there
Throughout our small galaxy.

I would like to live
In a place where everybody would give
Rather than take
Back further than the word freedom
All the way back to the Garden of Eden
With no fakers.

Jack Sams (13)
Sir Graham Balfour School

The Black Wolf

At midnight on the mountain,
The black wolf screeches his song,
Screeching at the silver moon,
Screeching all night long.

His demon eyes gleam at night,
As do his sharp white teeth,
He thumps his demon tail,
To the demon beat.

His sharp black claws,
Would rip your skin,
While the full moon shines,
But when the moon starts to wane,
He disappears from sight.

At midnight on the mountain,
The black wolf screeches his song,
Screeches at the silver moon,
Screeching all night long.

Amy Roe (12)
Sir Graham Balfour School

Teachermockery

(Inspired by 'Jabberwocky' by Lewis Carroll)

'Twas Tuesday and the Class 3B
Did laugh and giggle at the teacher
He was a supply and they wondered why
They'd been saddled with this useless creature.

Have fun with Sir, my friend
For we could cause the end
Of his teaching career with what we have here
So come, have some fun, my friend.

The blackboard squeaked
And 3B screeched at him and one another
And the teacher sighed and cried inside
And wished he'd stayed home with his mother.

Have fun with Sir, my friend
For we could cause the end
Of his teaching career with what we have here
So come, have some fun, my friend.

Pencils were hurled and rubbers were thrown
They scribbled on work that wasn't their own,
Windows were opened and books were no more
Turmoil thrived from ceiling to floor.

Have fun with Sir, my friend
For we could cause the end
Of his teaching career with what we have here
So come, have some fun, my friend.

Head teacher came in
Whole room was silent, several crept back to their seats,
'What's going on here?' he said, with a leer,
The class got detentions, oh dear!

Paige Softley (12)
Sir Graham Balfour School

What Should I Do?

Where should I go?
What should I do?
He whispered in my ear,
'I'm gonna get you.'

I could have told the teacher
But there's one tiny glitch
He said that if I ever did
He'd chuck me in a ditch!

He told me that I'm ugly
He said my mum's to blame
But everything he says is true
I'm really so ashamed.

I'm really ugly
I smell real bad
I've got no real talent
He said all this to make me sad.

Where should I go?
What should I do?
He whispered in my ear,
'I'm going to kill you!'

Kaitlyn Hamilton (12)
Sir Graham Balfour School

In The Eyes Of . . .

Crying for hours and hours,
Thinking about it over and over.
Blaming herself,
But what had she done?
Repeating the day's events,
Whilst huddled in a corner.
Rocking back and forth,
Miming the same words over.
To feel the pain that only she feels,
She fears the days ahead.
More,
Crying for hours and hours.
More,
Thinking about it over and over.
That's what it's like
For a victim
Of a bully.

Catherine Bate **(12)**
Sir Graham Balfour School

The Shun Of A Tramp

A mountain chill whispers into an innocent ear
Filling a pure soul with dread and fear.
Rustling of trees, the only sound
Bringing paranoia all around.
Constantly seeking to see another
A friend, a sister, an uncle, or brother.
Sitting alone in the corner I see
Many things I wanted to be.
Here I sit, making no sound
Forever longing to be found.
A passer-by to lend a hand
To my feet, there I stand.
But no one dares to help me now
As civilisation won't allow.
So here I am, for the rest of my days
In the corner, my tramp ways.
Hungry and cold, there I lie
Waiting for the day I die.

Rachael Maxwell Beckett Lane (13)
Sir Graham Balfour School

A Tramp's World

Cold
Cold
It's so cold
The streets are dirty
And I can't find anywhere to sleep

I see the warm, cosy houses
With their shimmering glow
My spirits are still low

I have the right to speak
No one listens
My eyes glisten
Tears fall down my face

I close my eyes and imagine
Imagine an old, cosy bed
I'll never have that luxury
Soon I'll be dead.

Harry Parker (13)
Sir Graham Balfour School

Giving A Voice To A Snail

I'm a very small snail
And I'm telling you my tale.

In gardens far and wide,
In greenery I hide.

I sneak behind the bushes,
I slide behind the trees,
I munch all the cabbages
And digest them with ease.

What a sorry little snail,
As he goes along his trail.

Looking for some food,
But he's not in the mood.

I don't eat everything that's good,
Snails eat rubbish too,
Garden pests aren't on my mind,
Because all I do is chew.

The snail is misunderstood,
No one knows he's doing good.

Of all the garden pests I know,
The snail's popularity continues to grow.

With hard shell,
Soft interior,
No one can say,
My friend's inferior.

Emily Raftery (13)
Sir Graham Balfour School

The Meaning Of Life Through My Eyes

The meaning of life through my eyes
Is short but simple
Happiness
Love
Understanding
And wisdom
You do your chores
You might get rewards
You find someone to love
To trust them forever
You live to be blessed
For pleasure, for peace
To be divine to God
And to you
And to me.

Joe Pelter (12)
Sir Graham Balfour School

Give A Voice . . .

Give a voice to someone who can't speak
Give a voice to a mouse who can only squeak
Give a voice to someone who can't say
'Please stay, don't go away'
Give a voice to someone so small
You won't be able to hear them at all
Give a voice to someone in need
Give them a quide dog, collar and lead
Give a voice to someone from far away
Who doesn't speak our language or know what to say
Give a voice to someone deep underground
A mole, a badger, you understand
Give a voice to someone who can't speak out
Let them have their say, let them shout!
Because today is the day
Today the people who have no voice
Can have their say.

Joe Thompson (12)
Sir Graham Balfour School

Cat

I sit in an alley day and night,
When people see my shadow I give them a fright,
When they realise that I'm just a cat,
They walk off and carry on with their chat.

Nobody cares about me or gives me food
And when they walk past I find it quite rude,
One day I decided to go to the street,
To see if there were any new cats I could meet,
It was far too busy for me
And there weren't any other cats that I could see.

All I want is a really good friend,
Someone that is a guardian angel
And helps me to the end,
I can't go on being lonely and sad,
If I had a friend it wouldn't be so bad.

Rebekah Trainer (13)
Sir Graham Balfour School

If I Could Turn Back Time

If I could turn back time
I'd change the world we live in.
Wars and fights would not exist,
Everyone would be forgiving.
There'd be no time for bombs and crimes,
Year on year would be good times.
There'd be no tears, just good fun living,
If I could turn back time
And change the world we live in.

Andrew McGuinness (12)
Sir Graham Balfour School

Meaning Of Life

A reaction occurs and the chemicals explode,
Meteors, stars and planets corrode,
Into spheres of mass, colours exposed,
Everything contained in the cosmos.
The Big Bang produced water and land,
More stars than there are grains of sand,
As people proved that science gave birth,
What are we doing, here on Earth?
The duties of humans, is to protect the world,
The mammals, reptiles, amphibians and bird,
Unfortunately, we have been too naïve,
As did the first two people, especially Eve.
Obviously, we are here to explore,
The solar system and much, much more,
Communicate with a galaxy from the Milky Way,
Mmm . . . chocolate, sorry for the delay.
Our duties as humans, to spread the population
And make our planet the strongest nation,
But killing us off, is a thing called Disease,
Why did God put it here? An explanation please!
What will go wrong? Will the world end?
As into a black hole we descend,
Global warming and pollution makes people worry,
This beautiful planet will end if we don't hurry!

Chris Talbot (13)
Sir Graham Balfour School

If I Could Go Back Into Time . . .

If I could go back in time,
I'd get rid of the pollution and grime.
Making the Earth a happier place,
So for our children it's not a disgrace.
That's if I could go back in time.

The creatures of this world would not die out,
From waste that's made a mess about.
Leaving the world a better place,
Which has not been destroyed by the human race.
That's if I could go back in time.

We would still have the technologies of today,
But these would not make carbon dioxide which would drift away.
Into the Earth's atmosphere,
Causing our natural shield to disappear.
That's if I could go back in time.

People would walk or ride on their bicycle more,
Instead of driving in the car to next door.
Making use of a fitter race,
Causing some diseases to disappear into space.
That's if I could go back in time.

If I could go back in time,
I'd get rid of pollution and grime.
Leaving the Earth to last longer
And not to die, burn and smoulder,
That's if I could go back in time.

Tom Wilson (14)
Sir Graham Balfour School

The Unheard Voice

'Strenuous heartbeats echo in my emaciated remains;
                                    but I never bemoan.
This is the immense affliction my existence contains,
This is my reality, this is my home:

But I never bemoan
My father: dying of starvation on the floor,
This is my reality, this is my home:
I feel the elixir of poverty tarnishing my continuation even more.

My father: dying of starvation on the floor,
My five brothers and sisters, imploring in an extensive exhaustion.
I feel the elixir of poverty tarnishing my continuation even more,
If I could alter my situation in a Faustian.

My five brothers and sister, imploring in an extensive exhaustion,
My accommodation: eligible for the accumulation of fragments.
If I could only alter my situation in a Faustian,
The innocence of our ethnicity: the blindness of the governments.

My accommodation: eligible for the accumulation of fragments,
Yearning for the diminutive of morsels.
The innocence of our ethnicity: the blindness of the governments,
Like many; I am melting in the embrace of the tunnels.

Yearning for the diminutive of morsels,
I am . . . fading.
Like many; I am melting in the embrace of the tunnels,
The judgement of hunger is excruciatingly invading.

I am . . . fading,
For I am few and you are many;
The judgement of hunger is excruciatingly invading,
We need help, any.'

Jessica Harding (13)
Sir Graham Balfour School

If I Could Turn Back Time

I was thinking last week, while I was walking,
Why do we have words and rhymes and sayings?
I thought to myself,
If I could turn back time,
I might just change one or two things,
Like sayings,
'Kill two birds with one stone',
How about having 'kill two mice with one stone'?
That's hardly different
And also words
I would go back in time
And maybe change 'because'
I mean, somebody, shall we say called George,
Might have been walking along the road and thought
I need a word that will fill in for 'that is why'
So you don't have to keep on saying it.
Then he would have thought,
I know, how about 'because'.
Why couldn't he have called it 'so' or 'maybe'.
I have got to tell you the truth,
If I could turn back time, I wouldn't change one thing,
Because (or so, or maybe) you can have it how you want it!

Katherine Carruthers (13)
Sir Graham Balfour School

We All Could

People say they'd go back,
Just to witness a historical event.

I would.

People say they'd go back,
To relive a great day in their lives.

I would.

People say they'd go back,
Just to stop a person from fatal danger.

I would.

People say they'd go back,
Just to meet their long ago ancestors.

I would.

People,
Some people,
Hardly any people,
No one,
Would go back in time to a dark place.
I would go back in time.

I would.

But I wouldn't go back to a dark place.

I would go back where horrible things happen.

And I wouldn't change them.

I couldn't
I wouldn't.

People say they'd go back
And rewrite history.

They wouldn't
You wouldn't
I wouldn't.

The fact is,
We can't go back in time.

The fact is,
We're still living in the past,
Where horrible things still happen.

The fact is,
We can change it.

I couldn't
You couldn't
They couldn't.

But:
We all could.

Lauren Alexander (14)
Sir Graham Balfour School

If I Could Turn Back Time

If I was able to turn back time
I'd travel to World War I
I'd reverse all the fighting, the blood and the hate
And make it completely gone

As I stare to the distance
And see the men die
All of the pain
Makes me cry

So I fly away after altering time
World War I has gone
Now to fix the World War II
And stop that atomic bomb

Hundreds and thousands of men on the plain
Lying and weeping in pain
Holding the letters from children and wives
Waving goodbye from the train

I'd fixed World War II
And fixed World War I
So I smiled and said
'My work here is done!'

Chris Basford (13)
Sir Graham Balfour School

In The Eyes Of A Ghost!

In the eyes of this ghost, I can see,
Sadness and despair,
Looking down on me.

In the eyes of this ghost, I can see,
Visions of the past,
So helpless and lonely.

Her mind is cold,
Her eyes only cry,
Because she never got to say goodbye.

In the eyes of this ghost, I can see,
The memories on how helpless and confused she was,
Confused about who she wished to be.

In the eyes of this ghost, I can see,
The person that she was
And who she wished to be.

Her mind is cold,
Her eyes only cry,
Because she never got to say goodbye.

In the eyes of this ghost, I can see,
Her looking down,
Upon what once was her family.

She sees me every night and day,
Wishing that she never did this to herself
Because she can't comfort me,
As she sees me confused and upset with dismay.

In the eyes of this ghost, I can see,
The thoughts of how angry and upset her parents are,
Upset about whom their daughter never got and never will be.

In this ghost, I can see, that her mind is cold,
Her eyes are crying tears of despair and regret,
These are the eyes of a dead smoker,
The eyes I will never forget.

Leah Boote (13)
Sir Graham Balfour School

Youth Of Today

There once was a boy, who lived on the streets,
He was eleven years old
And had to steal to eat.

He had no mum,
He had no dad,
This boy's life was very sad.

In a cardboard box he lived,
With his pillow,
Made of sticks.

He'd cry all night
And cry all day
And hope he'd find his parents someday.

One day he walked to the station
And boarded the train,
Started his journey again.

He got off the train,
Walked to find,
Somewhere to rest his weary mind.

He found a doorstep,
Of an unused bank,
Sat down quietly and asleep he sank.

He was woke up the next morning,
By the buzz of the streets
And was told to keep walking and follow his feet.

He cried like a baby,
Drove himself crazy,
Took out his knife
And threw away his life.

Danielle Pearce (13)
Sir Graham Balfour School

The Problems Of The World

God only gave us one world
So we may as well treat it well
The government promises to stop pollution
Is it telling the truth? It is hard to tell!

There are so many cars, the roads look like beehives
And it's only getting worse
Are we ruining our grandchildren's lives
Or are we going to act now and stop this?

Another problem is health
Wherever you go, you see obesity
It takes hours to find something healthy to eat
Because there are thousands of Chinese, Indian
And McDonald's take-aways in each city.

The world is full of problems
So do your bit and help us preserve our Earth
Or watch our world crumble
It's your choice.

God only gave us one world
Save it!

Rorigh Scott (13)
Sir Graham Balfour School

The Beautiful Sky

The sky's some beautiful colours
White when it goes cloudy
Grey when it's stormy and raining
As blue as the Mediterranean Sea

The great big, fluffy clouds
Clouds that are wispy and flat
Clouds that cover the whole sky
Then there's those that are fat

Clouds that are big and grey
Tell you, it's going to rain
If you are outside
Then it can be a real pain

When the sky has gone dark
And you look up in the night
The stars and the moon that you see
Oh, what a sight

On a nice summer's day
When the sky is a beautiful blue
There is a massive yellow sun
That's giving the light to you.

Adam Rhodes (13)
Sir Graham Balfour School

My Accident

I'm at the stables, waiting to ride
My horse is there, by my side
Here he is, tall and bold
He is the horse I long to hold.

As we walk quietly through
I think of the horse that I knew.

Now we're trotting through the lane
My horse is being quite a pain
He's getting in such a muddle
Cowering away from every puddle.

A man scares him with a hose
So up my horse rose
The man won't stop to look
He does not see that I am stuck.

What a day!
Then I fall and fade . . .

Away.

Beth Crutchley (13)
Sir Graham Balfour School

Icarus!

My heart was beating,
But I took the plunge,
The risk pulled off,
I was flying,
Soaring,
Gliding,
I swooped down,
To skim the water,
I pulled up,
Getting higher
And higher,
Trying to touch the sun,
I heard a frizzle
And looked to my side,
My wing was burnt
And I was falling,
Plummeting to the water,
The water's mouth swallowed me
And I was gone.

Drew Coleman (13)
Sir Graham Balfour School

My Best Friend

He is quite small,
With a fluffy white coat,
He responds when I call.

His nose is cold and wet,
When he is ill,
I take him to the vet.

He barks and barks,
When I take him out,
It is usually dark.

He must have been born in Scotland,
Because everyone calls him Scotty,
But his home is in England.

All his toys are soggy,
From biting,
This is because, he is my doggy!

Ben Priest (14)
Sir Graham Balfour School

Winter Morning

The sun shines out one cold winter's morning
As the birds start tweeting and eagles start soaring
As the foxes come out, the night creatures go in
And the trees grow taller as the snow grows smaller
The peaceful night grows into a long morning
And the day starts off as a cold winter's morning.

Nico Brice (14)
Sir Graham Balfour School

Icarus

I carus is flying
C ruising through the air
A lways rising
R ising to the sun
O h no, the
S un is melting the wax

W ill
I carus
L ive any
L onger?

D iving
I nto his
E verlasting watery grave.

Adam Thorpe (13)
Sir Graham Balfour School

Why?

People have to deal
With fear, hate and prejudice
Why?

We have to live
Through war, death and destruction
Why?

We watch people suffer every day . . .
We do something about it,
Not enough . . .
Why?

We could do more
So why don't we?

A single question . . .
Why?
Millions of answers . . .
Why?
Not one is good enough . . .
Why?

Eleanor Huguet (13)
Sir Graham Balfour School

Planet Zeth

Planet Zeth of rage and hate
Where all they do is fight!
The people there cannot feel love
But feel misery and discontent,
Where all you hear is guns and bombs,
You no longer see the birds and bees
But people screaming of fear,
Even the king will fight to the death
And all that people say is goodbye or goodnight,
It will finish when one person is left
And has killed and shed all the blood
He may be king of Zeth, but in life, he will also face death!

Aiden Taylor (13)
Sir Graham Balfour School

Communication

A poem,
A story,
A book,
Or a dream.

Pen to the paper,
Eyes or the mind,
Pictures,
Or words.

Sign language,
Expressions,
Sounds,
Or touch.

A feeling,
An emotion,
A thought,
Or an idea.

A look,
A word,
An action,
Or a surprise.

A message,
A silence,
A presence,
Or a knowing.

So many ways.

Megan Holding (13)
Sir Graham Balfour School

The Snowy Mountain

The snowy mountain
Climbed by no one but the wind
Magnificent, powerful, gigantic
Like a skyscraper touching Heaven
Like a snow palace
It makes me feel special
Like an extraordinary parcel
That everybody wants to open
Reminds us how wonderful
The Earth is!

Hannah Robinson (13)
Sir Graham Balfour School

Tears From The Graveyard

In the spine-tingling graveyard
With the mossed-over gravestones
Wraith-like figures hover
Around the churchyard.

Appearing to be deadly
These creatures are quite harmless
For they mourn to be amongst the living
For they are not

Forlorn and weary
They seek to give comfort
To those left behind
In sorrow and pain

Searching for loved ones
Whose visits are less frequent
Their desire to rejoin them
Will always be in vain.

Chris Jolliffe
Sir Graham Balfour School

The Storm

Gloomy clouds form
The sky darkens
The sound of rain is heard
A storm is brewing

Animals seek shelter
They scramble across the dirt
Showing their young ones to safety
Suddenly, comes the crack of thunder

Lightning strikes a tree
It falls
Knocking other trees down like dominoes
The storm is carving a path of destruction

As if nothing had happened
The sun innocently peeps out
And shines into the forest
Showing the mayhem that has taken place

Water gently drips from the leaves
The animals come back out
All that happened is forgotten
And the storm moves to strike elsewhere.

Ben Evans (13)
Sir Graham Balfour School

Icarus And Daedalus

King Minos had a plan,
He needed to capture a man,
An inventor to build and design,
A labyrinth so fine.

Daedalus was the man for the job,
King Minos with lies, he did fob.
Said once the job was done,
Said Daedalus was free, as was his son.

But the deal was not kept,
Daedalus could have wept,
But instead he devised a plan
And made wings with a great span.

He met Icarus at the top of the tower,
'Son, with these wings you have great power,
But do not fly too close to the sun,
If the wax melts, it will be no fun.

Nor fly too low,
Because the sea is a foe,
The current will pull you in,
Fly between the sun and sea to win.'

Daedalus and Icarus started to fly,
Soaring so very high,
Icarus got carried away
And the price he had to pay.

The wax holding his wing
Melted, feathers began to ping.
He was falling fast,
Into the sea he was cast.

Icarus so sadly drowned,
His body, Daedalus eventually found,
He was buried by his dad,
An ending so very sad.

Jake Bartlett (13)
Sir Graham Balfour School

If . . .

If grass is green
And sky is blue,
Sand is golden yellow.

If playing is fun
And running is quick,
Then walking is very slow.

If bricks are heavy
And feathers are light,
Then glass is in-between.

If clocks tell the time
And paintings tell the past,
So then, what tells the future?

If God made the Earth
And Adam helped make Eve,
Then the world is a place of paradise.

If fish live in the sea
And humans live on land,
Then where do the rest of the world live?

If I wrote this poem
And I thought of this,
Then what gave me these ideas?

Jessica Wright (13)
Sir Graham Balfour School

Football Is Life

Football is life!
I play it every day,
Get my football and play,
I try to do it my way.

I travel the country for a game,
Two games are never the same,
The team I play for is Port Vale,
We put our hearts out and don't fail,
I go into my own world, like a fairy tale.

I know so many tricks,
Also known as flicks,
In a way I'm an expressionist,
Also being a perfectionist.

So football,
Playing it - so cool,
So think about it
And give the ball one good hit.

Callum Whittaker (13)
Sir Graham Balfour School

If I Were Pi

(Inspired by the book, 'Life of Pi' by Yann Martel)

If I were Pi
Trapped in a boat
With the sea and the sky
I'd go completely insane

With four animals, dangerous maybe
Not much food, but rations
Great white sharks lie deep beneath the sea
No friendly face, it's just me

They're picking them off, one by one
Zebra's gone, orang-utan gone
Left is a man-eating tiger that weighs a ton
The hyena is getting restless

There is no more food, I'm in a spin
The hyena's hungry
So is the tiger, breathing out and in
I'm worried, so worried, what am I going to do?

An island, I'm saved at last
Hyena's dead, tiger's fed
Me and tiger cling to the mast
For the island is a watery grave

So long my friend at the end of the boat
I will miss you very much
Such a long time we have stayed afloat
Just me and you together
Now you have gone, I'll remember you forever.

Rosy Crawley (13)
Sir Graham Balfour School

The Hockey Match

My skates glide fast beneath me
The roar of the crowd fills my ears
Amongst the noise I hear the cheers
The ice is fast

He moves towards us, skating hard
Now's his chance, he draws back his stick
Takes a shot, but our goalie's too quick
The ice is fast

It's our turn now, our chance to shine
With the speed of a stallion we charge ahead
The chants of the crowd fill my head
The ice is fast

Thirty seconds to go, just one goal would win it
Pulses are racing, hearts beating fast
I take my shot
Glory at last!

David Furber (13)
Sir Graham Balfour School

Drawing

Drawing, hard for some
Drawing, easy for others
Drawing, a way to show emotion
Drawing, a way to speak without words
Drawing, brings happiness to many
Drawing, brings frustration to many
Drawing, attractive and pretty
Drawing, ugly and disgusting
Drawing, so simple and basic
Drawing, so complicated and mysterious
Drawing, all over the world
Drawing, so much of it known
Drawing, so much to be found
Drawing, being made all the time
Drawing, worth lots of money
Drawing, worth lots in sentiments
Drawing, drawing, drawing.

Lloyd James (13)
Sir Graham Balfour School

What Mum And Dad Said

Mum said put the kettle on
I said it didn't fit

Dad said turn over the telly
It didn't look so good backwards

Mum said put the cat out
I asked who set it on fire

Dad said run the bath
I asked him where to

Mum said unpack the dishwasher
I asked where it had been

Mum said act sensible
I said I failed drama

Dad said buy the fish a tank
I couldn't drive it home though

Mum said feed the dog
I asked her what to!

Jennie Williams (13)
Sir Graham Balfour School

Books - A Key To Your Learning

B lurb, the plot to the book
O ld and new, they go through generations
O nomatopoeia, a word that sounds like the thing it describes,
Used a lot in books
K nowledge and learning
S imilies, a figure of speech in which one thing is directly likened
To another, used a lot in books

When you open a book
You open a whole new world . . .

Jonathon Ackroyd (13)
Sir Graham Balfour School

By Your Side

When you think you're worthless,
In the way when you're around,
Stop drowning in self-pity
And pick yourself up off the ground.

When you think no one would cry,
If you dropped dead on the spot,
Open your eyes and see before you,
All the friends that you have got.

When you think the world is cruel
And life is so unfair,
You can always depend on your family,
Because they really do care.

And when you need someone to talk to,
When all your tears have been cried,
You can always come to me,
'Cause I'll be by your side.

Joanne Mansfield (13)
Sir Graham Balfour School

My World

My world is just a dream
Nothing is real
As I sit and think about it
My head starts to reveal.

All the things around me
New or old they can be
Nothing means anything
My world is completely free.

My life is just starting
As my head grows high
I thank all the people
And the people who made me cry.

Everyone has made me think
Now my life is real
God bless all you people
My life is on the heal.

Natalie Dix (12)
Sir Graham Balfour School

Stalker

The stalker lurked behind a tree

A misty gloom, hung damp and low
Hiding what it did not want to show

The stalker lurked behind a tree

The school bell rang, I was free
I leapt and shouted a big, *yippee!*

The stalker lurked behind a tree

I ran to the park as fast as I could
As fast as a cheetah, then I crashed into the mud

The stalker lurked behind a tree

With a silly grin on my face I stood upright
I heard a *snap* and gave a fright

The stalker lurked behind a tree

I set off running, away from the noise
But then I heard footsteps
Getting louder and louder
The lush, green garden grass
Came as a blur
And I heard his breath, sticky-hot on my neck
There was a piercing scream
Coming from my own mouth

Then . . .
Silence

The dagger in my back
Burnished crimson with my blood
Felt like an icy cold, steely chill
Running through my flesh
I turned around for the last time
And saw
The stalker, still lurking behind that tree.

Charlie Dennis (12)
Sir Graham Balfour School

If I Could Go Back In Time

If I could go back in time
I would change what I did
I didn't mean to hurt her
And I don't know why I did

If I could go back in time
I would change what I did
I would stop myself from
Hurting the person who bullied me

If I could go back in time
I would change what I did
I would make no bullies
So then it wouldn't have happened

If I could go back in time
I would change what I did
I would talk to my younger self
And not do what I did

If I could go back in time
I would change what I did
It's all because of me
That now Regina's dead!

Lauren Masters (12)
Sir Graham Balfour School

Why Me?

Why me?
Scared and terrified, all alone
Avoiding everyone on my own
Why me?
Covering up my face, very ashamed
Is it me who should be blamed?
Why me?
I see them now, looking at me
Run away, I need to be free
Why me?
They start chasing, my heart racing
I turn around, now they're gaining
Why me?
They grab my shoulder, pull out a knife
It can't be, is it the end of my life?
Why me?
I'm in need of somebody!

Hannah Guildford (12)
Sir Graham Balfour School

The View Of A Victim Being Bullied

I can't go back, not to that place
Where that Miranda's always in my face
Spitting and smacking
Staring and glaring
Then it gets worse
Nicking my money, thinking it's funny
Why me, what's wrong with me?
She takes 50p out of my pocket
Saying it's going in her piggybank
My heart sank and sank
I felt like crying
She slapped me round the face
Telling me to shut up
I wanted to go home
So my mum could take the tears away
And tell me I never had to go back there
Not for even one more single day
Instead, she tells me not to cry
And try and stand on my own two feet
I always try to defeat, but I never can
I just hope one day, the tears will go away
And that Miranda will leave me in peace to play.

Olivia Roberts (12)
Sir Graham Balfour School

The Bully

I don't know why I do it
I just do
I have hurt everyone I ever knew

I hurt her
Because she's a nerd
But really I'm jealous of her

I don't have any mates
I'm doomed to be a loner
It's my fate

My mum doesn't love me
I don't know my dad
This is why I'm always sad

So no one I know
Should be happy
Why should they
If I can't be?

Natalie Davies (12)
Sir Graham Balfour School

My Cat

My cat is very stupid,
My cat is very fat
And when my cat comes in the house,
He often brings a rat.
When my cat gets hungry,
He eats his food with greed,
I often think that he would eat,
Carrots, peas and swede.
My cat is black and white,
Him and his mum fight
And when he gets his claws out,
He will scratch with all his might.

Russell Taylor (13)
Sir Graham Balfour School

Poetry, Poetry

Poetry, poetry, it hasn't got a single rule
And all you need for a poem,
Is imagination, that's the only tool.

Poetry, poetry, it doesn't need to be rhyming,
It doesn't need to have any similies
And it doesn't need to have any timing.

Poetry, poetry, you can do whatever you want,
Because there aren't any rules,
You can even write in any font.

Evan Clark (12)
Sir Graham Balfour School

Driving Down The Motorway

D riving down the motorway
R unning up the miles with glee
I n the warm summer breeze
V ehicles surround me, all around me
I see the sun shining
N owhere near the night
G rey clouds nowhere to be seen

D evishly hot, the sun shines with might
O ut of the window, I see cars driving by
W ith one more look, I see a lone sheep
N o one beside him

T o see him grazing on a grassed heap
H ills in the distance
E dging closer

M otorbikes speed along
O nly we are going where we want
T he only thing slowing us is traffic
O h, what a bore
R ailways are much quieter
W hilst motorways are more scenic
A nd I think we are there
Y es we are!

Ryan Barnes (13)
Sir Graham Balfour School

It Could Be A Better Place

The world could be a better place,
Where people don't care about your race
And no one will need to cover their face,
You know it could be a better place.

You know we could make the grass grow greener,
Just pick up litter and make the world cleaner,
You know everyone should be keener,
Just make the world a better place.

The world could be a better place,
Where people don't care about your race
And no one will need to cover their face,
You know it could be a better place.

Now listen to what I am about to say,
The world could be in a better way,
There is no price you have to pay,
You can make a change - start today!

The world could be a better place,
Where people don't care about your race
And no one will need to cover their face,
You know it could be a better place.

You know the world is full of pollution,
So that means we need to find a solution!

Joe Hewitt (12)
Sir Graham Balfour School

Questions

I think
Why is the sky blue?
What makes cows moo?
Why do babies like peekaboo
And who made my shoe?
But to be honest, I don't know

I think
Why do we eat food?
What gives us moods?
Why do people get sued
And what makes people rude?
But to be honest, I don't know

I have one last thing to say
What made me ask these things today?

Megan McDonald (12)
Sir Graham Balfour School

Young Writers Information

We hope you have enjoyed reading this book - and that you will continue to enjoy it in the coming years.

If you like reading and writing poetry drop us a line, or give us a call, and we'll send you a free information pack.

Alternatively if you would like to order further copies of this book or any of our other titles, then please give us a call or log onto our website at www.youngwriters.co.uk

Young Writers Information
Remus House
Coltsfoot Drive
Peterborough
PE2 9JX

(01733) 890066